So many
Everests

So many Everests

FROM CEREBRAL PALSY
TO CASUALTY CONSULTANT

———————————

DIANA AND VICTORIA WEBSTER

LION

This edition published by Lion Books
an imprint of
Lion Hudson plc
Wilkinson House, Jordan Hill Road,
Oxford OX2 8DR, England
www.lionhudson.com/lion
ISBN 978 0 7459 5595 7
e-ISBN 978 0 7459 5761 6

A catalogue record for this book is available from the
British Library

Printed and bound in Great Britain, August 2012, LH26

To Mike

CONTENTS

DIANA'S STORY

CHAPTER 1

It was the rubber boots that puzzled me. Why was the doctor in the room wearing rubber boots?

As he came to my side, I asked: 'Why are you wearing boots?'

He looked surprised, then embarrassed and said: 'The blood...'

Blood? Wading through blood? Oh. I supposed foggily that there possibly was a lot of blood in childbirth, though I hadn't thought about it before.

Then another of the tidal waves hit me, rolling down my body like an unstoppable surge.

'Puss!' said the Finnish doctor. 'Puss!'

I pushed – or tried to.

'More hard! Puss! More hard!'

It couldn't be harder, I thought. Not possibly. Then the wave stopped as if it had met the shoreline. Almost immediately, another rolled in.

This time the doctor was not saying 'Puss' but telling me the opposite.

'Hold back! Hold back!'

But how could you hold back the sea? My body was no longer mine but in the grip of something much stronger, over which I had no control at all but which simply took me over and did what it liked with me. I was as powerless as King Canute had been to stop the waves rolling in.

Finally they stopped of themselves and it was as if I had been thrown up floundering onto the shore, breathless, too tired to do anything but lie back exhausted. Had I had a baby?

'It's a little girl, Mrs Webster,' said the doctor.

Everyone seemed to be very busy somewhere. Didn't babies cry when they were born? They did in the films.

'Where's the baby?' I asked

'We must take the baby away.'

'Why?'

'There is lack of oxygen. It was difficult.'

And that was how my daughter, an otherwise perfect and healthy baby, was born with brain damage.

It was nobody's fault.

It was Good Friday. The hospital was under-staffed. My regular gynaecologist was attending a conference. The baby was too early. None of this was supposed to happen. It was nobody's fault; there was nobody really to blame. It would perhaps have been easier if we had been able to blame someone: perhaps the doctor who had been on duty that night and who failed to give me the Caesarean which these days I would certainly have had. But the hospital was short-staffed. Thirty-five was not so very old to have a first baby even in 1965, and I was healthy and fit. It's perhaps understandable that the doctor did not think it entirely necessary.

Not that I understood anything at the time. I had of course read the books available for new mothers-to-be; I had gone to classes, practised the breathing. But it was all a bit like my early sex education, when I had read an extremely detailed book called a Medical Dictionary of Sex. As a result, I was more primed than most with knowledge of sexual deviations and unusual positions and practices, but what had somehow escaped me was the basic information about the essential actions and sensations. The same was true now about childbirth. The fact was that I had really had no idea what to expect either in having sex for the first time or in having a baby. What's more, I couldn't ask now. I was in Finland, in a Finnish maternity hospital and my Finnish was very limited. The ability to ask where the station is or to buy a litre of milk in another language does not equip one for describing the type and severity of one's contractions in labour or anything else I needed to explain or ask at that moment.

In the early hours of Good Friday, Mike had taken me in to the maternity hospital, where he had left me outside the labour ward. Husbands were not allowed to come further. I lay on a hard, narrow, rexene-covered hospital bed in a dark indentation in a corridor with a very thin cotton blanket over me. Occasionally another woman would be wheeled beside me. The women never spoke anything else but Finnish, so we exchanged little but groans. Then one by one the women would be wheeled away and I would go on lying there alone. At what seemed long intervals a nurse would come to ask me how I was doing – or so I supposed, because the only English-speaking nurse eventually went off duty. Had my waters broken? I didn't know, because I didn't know what to expect – the books had not gone into details – was it a tiny trickle or was it a flood? At any rate apparently my contractions were somehow never satisfactory enough, because I was never wheeled away.

The morning became the afternoon; the afternoon became night; the light in the corridor became dimmer; it was impossible to read or to do anything but lie and wait for the next searing contraction. At first I had rung

Mike from time to time to tell him that there was no news, but the only telephone was a long walk down the corridor. Eventually I became too tired to make the effort. I longed for him. I longed for a friend. I longed for anyone who could speak English. I have never felt so lonely, so desolate and so helpless. To be bereft of the ability to make yourself understood is to be no longer in control of your life, to be disempowered.

At last the moment came when I was wheeled away to another room. It was in darkness, with light only showing from a small strip of window at the top of the door. I traced the glint of metal, the outline of lighting equipment over and above a slab a few feet away from mine. The Delivery Room? Now, I thought, now I will have the baby. But nothing at all happened, only the recurring contractions. Presumably they were still not satisfactory. To me, however, they were intolerable. Was this what labour was like? Was it always so terrible? The books had made it sound fairly easy, and I had no comparison to make.

'How are you, Mrs Webster?'

It was the Finnish doctor on night duty, someone I had not met before.

'Not good. Can I have something for the pain? I don't think I can stand it.'

'It is normal, Mrs Webster.'

'It can't be. Please.'

'No. I am sorry.'

'Why not? Why not?'

'It can be not good. Not good for the baby. You must be strong.'

'Please!'

'No. Sorry.'

He went, leaving me alone in the dark. I looked at the dim outline of the windows. Could I open them? Throw myself out and end this? But I felt too weak even to get up.

The next time the doctor came in I was screaming. This time he gave me an injection and things became more manageable again and a little vague.

Then bright, blinding lights. I was in yet another room, lying on yet another green-rexened slab. That was when I saw the doctor's rubber boots.

So the baby was at last delivered, and taken away immediately before I even saw it. Not for me those touching scenes in the films where the midwife delivers the naked baby wrapped in a towel into its smiling mother's arms and she looks down with relief, pride and joy. I still lay on the slab, waiting.

After a time the doctor trudged over to me, still in his rubber boots.

'What is the baby's name?' he asked.

'What...? We haven't got a name yet.'

'We must have a name.'

'Why?'

The doctor hesitated. 'The baby must be...' He didn't know the word, 'A priest must give a name.'

'You mean baptize her?'

'Yes. Baptize.'

But that meant... Surely that must mean...

We had thought we had plenty of time for names: a situation like this had never crossed our minds. We had giggled over the choice, thinking up names that were not really for people but sounded as if they could be: Semolina, Forsythia, Rubella. I remembered now that Mike had also joked about calling the baby something beginning with V – then she would be able to have a car with her initials on the front: VW.

What girl's name began with V? Violet – no, no! Victoria? I'd had a great-aunt called Victoria. It was a pretty name, optimistic too: V for Victory, we'd said as children in the war. What would Mike think of the name? I didn't want to decide our baby's name without him.

'Victoria,' I said.

The doctor went away and I continued to lie on the slab. Some time later the midwife came in with a white bundle.

'Your daughter, Mrs Webster.'

My daughter. She was in swaddling clothes. I had only ever seen swaddling clothes or heard the expression in medieval pictures of the Christ child but I recognized them at once. Tightly wrapped, almost like a tiny shroud, with only her pale face visible in its wrappings and a wisp of black hair. The midwife did not give her to me to hold. I reached up a slow finger, drew it very gently down the little length of her face. Her skin was like warm silk. Victoria.

'Hello, little one,' I said.

Then she was taken away.

CHAPTER 2

I dozed fitfully in my bed in the maternity ward until the morning began to grey. They had put me in a separate room, so again I was alone. Sometimes I was wakened by the distant cry of a baby. Not mine, though.

Finally the events of the night began to return and I woke up for good. I felt strangely detached, as if I had never had a baby, but my fingertips still remembered a warm, silky skin. They had taken it away to give it more oxygen, they had said. Surely oxygen was something essential? What did a lack of oxygen? Would it damage the baby and, if so, how? Where was Mike? I wanted Mike.

'When can I see my husband?'

The nurse spoke some English. 'In visiting hours, Mrs Webster.'

'When's that?'

'Between one and two o'clock.'

'But that's another six hours away! Can't I see him before that?'

'I am sorry, no, Mrs Webster. They are the rules.'

'Can I telephone him then?'

'Yes, of course. I will bring a telephone to your room.'

The phone didn't come. Gingerly, I got up – the birth had torn me and I had had to have several stitches, so sitting down had to be done carefully, balancing on the side of one buttock. I went out into a white corridor and walked along to find a nurse or a phone. As I did, I passed a long glass window in the left-hand wall. I looked through. Babies. Rows of baby faces peeking out of swaddling bands in their cots like tiny Egyptian mummies. Some I could see were crying, crumpling up the folds of their faces and opening and shutting their mouths, some squidging a grimace, some giving a delicate little yawn, others sleeping tranquilly. Some had tufts of black hair showing, some had a faint yellow down, some were totally bald. None of them was my baby. I returned to my room.

After a long, long while someone came with a telephone. I dialled our number, but Mike wasn't at home.

Suddenly I felt impelled to do something, anything that might help the baby. So far I had been, it seemed, totally helpless, a mere birth-machine in the hands of others who had decided everything for me and had finally removed my baby. That baby was somewhere here, though, in this very hospital, in an oxygen tent. Was she still alive?

Then I remembered Pelle. Pelle was a consultant at one of the children's hospitals in Helsinki and was a friend of my mother's – wouldn't a special hospital be better than here? In any event, there would be someone who knew us at the other hospital, to whom the baby would not just be any baby but our baby.

It was a Saturday and I prayed that he would be there, knowing that doctors often did not work at weekends, but Pelle was on duty. He was always a laconic man and no more so than on the telephone. He just listened and said: 'Right. I'll get her over here right away.'

He didn't offer comment or sympathy – he just acted –

and I lay back on my bed with a huge sense of relief. She'd be all right now – Pelle would see to it.

I waited through the long, long time until visiting hours. At last Mike opened the door and came over to hug me.

'I'm so sorry, sweetie,' he said.

'You know?'

He nodded. 'They phoned me.'

'They gave her four points at birth, they said.'

'What does that mean?'

'Apparently they give points to babies when they are born. As if they were in a health race. Ten points to the best babies.'

'Ah.' We looked at each other.

I said: 'I got through to Pelle. He said he would get her sent over straight away to the Children's Hospital and look after her.'

'I know. He told me and I went over to see her.'

'You've seen her?'

'Such a pretty baby, sweetie. Lots of black hair.'

'I couldn't really see. She was almost all covered up when they showed her to me.'

'A lovely baby. Clever old you.'

It was much, much later that Mike told me that when he saw her in the Intensive Care Unit she was having a convulsion. She was in a domed glass case, like a Victorian trophy, with a tube in her nose; while he was there she turned rigid, blue. He never said either then or later what his feelings were about the whole thing but just did everything he could to make me feel better.

'Look, I've brought you this.'

He held up an unsightly dark red rubber ring, which he proceeded to blow up.

'What...?' I said.

'It's for people with piles, but I thought it would do for you.'

I giggled and tried sitting on it. From then on, for my three or four days in hospital I was the envy of many a precariously buttock-balancing mum. I asked a nurse if it wouldn't be a good idea to have a supply that women could borrow.

She shook her head disapprovingly. 'No, it is not good for mothers,' she said.

'Why on earth not?'

'They heal better with no... no cushion.'

I didn't believe her for a moment – 'They just haven't thought of it,' I said to myself, and continued to sit comfortably. There seemed in fact to be a general feeling in Finnish hospitals at that time that pain was essential to childbirth, perhaps because of the famous Finnish *sisu*, a word which expresses a kind of stoical persistence in the face of all hardships. An Italian friend of mine, who had a baby a couple of years later in a private hospital, asked as I had for something to help the pain, but was told curtly and unsympathetically: 'You can't expect to have a baby without pain. Finnish women don't.'

Attitudes have fortunately changed since then and Finland is as advanced as any other western country in pain relief. Changes have happened elsewhere too: husbands are regularly present at the actual birth and there would be no rules about visiting hours for a husband to visit a wife whose baby had been taken to intensive care or who had died. But it was not so in 1965 – and worse was to come.

A couple of days later I woke up to a soaking wet nightie and sheets. I couldn't think at first what had happened. There was a familiar and yet unfamiliar smell, slightly sour. Milk? Yes, but... Again the books hadn't mentioned this aspect of it – I didn't know you *leaked*. There had only been pictures of a happy mother and a blissfully sucking baby. I hadn't realized either that you could have milk without having the baby. It seemed so unfair.

When the nurse finally came, she said: 'Ah, your milk is in, Mrs Webster. I bring a bowl.'

A *bowl*? What would I do with a bowl? Have the milk with cornflakes?

The nurse came back with a largish metal bowl.

'Here you are,' she said. 'You must – express – the milk.'

'Express?' I asked, baffled.

She made movements of pulling at her own nipple. I realized that she meant I must milk myself. Like a cow, I thought. After all, that's what happened to cows, wasn't it: they had a calf, then the milk came for the calf, then the calf was taken away but they kept on milking the cow. I suppose they leak too if they aren't milked. Poor bloody cows.

'I show you,' said the nurse. 'It is easy.'

She put her finger and her thumb on either side of my nipple with a squeezing motion and a spray of milk shot out into the bowl.

'Now you try.'

It had looked easy. However, it was surprisingly difficult to master, to find exactly where to press, the precise movement of the fingers needed and the critical pressure. After I had tried and failed several times, the nurse said: 'I get you – machine.'

She returned with a metal instrument with a small cup which she clamped to my breast. The milk began to come out again. I remembered those rows of cows in the milking sheds with metal pumps attached to their teats. No, I would not be a dairy cow.

'Stop, please,' I said. 'I want to try again myself.'

And finally I did get the hang of it. A steady stream of milk squirted in a narrow spray against the side of the metal bowl. I recalled the sound. As a child on a farm in the summers in England I had watched the farmhand milking a cow by hand: siss! siss! siss! into the metal bucket. I also remembered a painting I had seen of a Madonna and Baby, one of the thousands, by – whom? some Italian? – but the only one I had ever seen where the milk was coming out of Mary's breast in a fine spray of misty white. Well, at least that artist had seen the real thing and recorded it, although I did not feel a bit Madonna-ish.

'Why do I have to do it?' I asked the nurse. 'What's the point when I haven't got a baby?'

'Then you make more milk. It do not stop. So then when Baby come home, you can feed her.'

'Oh yes!' I said eagerly. 'I want to do that.'

'And before baby is well, you can take your milk to hospital each day.'

'But would she get it?' I asked. 'Would it go to *her*?'

'Oh yes,' said the nurse, though whether she really knew or not I couldn't tell. 'Or,' she added, 'you can sell it.'

'*Sell* it?'

'Yes. Mother's milk is very expensive. You can take it to shop. They give you good price.'

I saw her point – yes, there must be a demand for mother's milk, probably very sick babies might be prescribed it or some mothers who could not feed their own child might want it – but the idea off selling it still appalled me. When I thought about it, though, I saw it could be a source of real income to the very poor, as it had been to them in days gone by, when the rich mostly did not feed babies themselves but farmed them out to a wet-nurse in the country, for good or ill.

After this, I industriously milked myself, telling myself that if – when – the baby was returned to us I would be able to feed her and, until then, I could send her the milk daily. I knew that it probably did not make any difference which baby got my milk or whose milk my baby got, but subconsciously I felt it did: it would be a distant bond with

22

her, part of me going to her. Besides, it was the only thing I could do for her, the only way in which I could help.

Then the day came for me to leave hospital. I had read the notice in my room: Mothers and babies should leave the hospital between the hours of 11 and 12. A member of the family or some other person should come to the hospital to fetch them.

Mothers and babies... Or, as it turned out, mothers without their babies as well. When Mike came to collect me, we walked down the corridors together. Other husbands were there too. They had bundles in shawls in their arms or were carrying the tiny bundles in carry-cots, mothers shooting anxious glances at their men in case they dropped them. All were excited, happy, relieved. Mike and I held hands tightly.

He had to leave me on a bench by the exit while he went to fill in forms. I watched the parents and their babies, heard snatches of conversation.

'Look, Kati, it's your baby sister!'

'Isn't she tiny!'

'Do you think she's warm enough?'

The tears began to dribble down my face. I had not cried until that moment. Somehow, up to then, everything had seemed slightly unreal, but now the reality was made visible: others had babies; I did not.

Why, I wondered then and wonder now, had nobody considered the cruelty of making people like us leave at the same time as the others? Couldn't the rules have been bent to allow at least half an hour in between? Would it have been so much more difficult to administer? And why had nobody protested?

Tears were also in Mike's eyes as we left and we rode home in a taxi with our hands clasped painfully tight, almost without words.

CHAPTER 3

Fortunately there was no pretty-papered little room waiting for us with a frilled cot and brightly swinging baby toys. We had no extra room in our flat and we had both been working far too hard before Easter to get around to preparing anything very much. 'We'll see what's needed and get it then' had been our philosophy.

So the flat was exactly as it had been and we returned to our lives almost as if there had never been a baby at all.

The next day Mike had to go off to work, although rather ironically I was still on maternity leave. I was trying to do things around the flat somewhat aimlessly when the phone rang. It was Pelle from the Children's Hospital.

'About your baby,' he said. My stomach tightened.

'I'm glad to say she is out of danger now, but we will have to keep her here for a bit.'

Before I could relax, he added: 'But there's just one thing you ought to know.'

'Yes?'

'As you know, your baby had to be given artificial respiration at birth...' *Did she? Did she? They hadn't said.* 'And that meant she suffered an oxygen deficiency.'

'Yes?'

'We did the usual tests and found some blood in her spinal cord.'

'Yes?'

'So,' he hesitated slightly, 'that means she will have suffered some brain damage.'

'Brain damage, yes.'

'Of course it's far too soon to tell where the damage is precisely.'

'When – when would one know?'

'Probably not until she is about two. And of course,' he hurried on, 'it may be nothing very serious. It may be that she just won't be very good at maths – or music – it depends exactly which part of the brain is damaged.'

'I see,' I said. 'But might – might she be affected – mentally?'

'As I said,' Pelle said, avoiding the direct answer, 'it's far too early even to guess, so it's best not to think about it too much now. Wait till she's about two. But I wanted to tell you.'

He rang off after telling me that we could probably have the baby home in a week or two.

I couldn't think about that, however. The only thing I could think of, the two words that pounded in my ears, were 'brain damage'. I was sitting on the edge of my bed and stayed there, thinking of all the possible implications. I tried to concentrate on the other part of what Pelle had said – maybe she would just not be good at maths or something. My mind wouldn't stay there but kept on going back to those words 'brain damage' and 'serious'. What did 'serious' mean? That she might not be able to walk, talk, eat – *think*? Oh no, not that, please not that!

Images ran through my mind: she might grow up drooling, gibbering, wetting her bed all her life, helpless, not able to feed herself. And I would be the one who would have to look after her! I would be tied all my life to a drooling idiot! I knew I wasn't supposed to feel like that about anyone, let alone my own child. I knew I should feel compassion, pity. But I didn't think I could cope with those images I had conjured up. I felt I wasn't unselfish enough or brave enough. Desperately I prayed to God to give me the strength to bear this appalling burden.

I threw myself across my bed, consumed by terror, anguish and shame, and beat the bedclothes with my fists, my body racked by tearing sobs.

Gradually I quietened. I was immensely glad that Mike had not been there to see and hear this screaming, uncontrolled, selfish self and I was determined he should never know. It was a passing madness, because I would have to cope: other people did, so why shouldn't I?

So when Mike returned from work, there was no sign of my tears and we just hugged each other quietly. I was able to say calmly: 'I heard from Pelle today – he says she's out of danger and we can have her back in a week or so.'

'Wonderful, sweetie.'

'Oh and he said they'd found some blood in her spinal fluid, so there'll be some brain damage – not necessarily serious, Pelle said.'

'Yes, he told me. It'll be all right, you'll see.'

'Yes.'

It seemed that he and Pelle had talked while I was still in the hospital, but they had both thought it was better for me to hear the news after I had got home. So Mike had known about the blood and the brain damage and once again he had had to bear alone what must have been his pain and his fears too. Had he had the same feelings as I had? I shall never know.

At work at the university all our colleagues had now of course learned about the baby from Mike or on the grapevine. That evening our Assistant Professor of English, Tauno Mustanoja, rang up to say how sorry he was and could he do anything?

'It's sweet of you, Tauno, but I don't think there is anything anybody can do.'

'Well, at least let me drive you to the Children's Hospital when you next go – I know you haven't got a car. When are you going?'

'They said we could go tomorrow, but…'

'Then I insist. What time should you be there?'

And Tauno continued to insist, even though we did not really want a third person along on this special occasion when we both first saw our daughter together. But sometimes it is important to let other people feel that they are doing something to help, so we finally agreed.

We need not have worried about Tauno: he was very tactful.

'I'll wait outside,' he said. 'I'd like to see her, though, so perhaps you could come and fetch me after a while.'

I suppose I had expected to go into the ward and see her lying in an oxygen tent, as Mike had. But we were not allowed in. Wise, of course, because of bacteria, but deeply frustrating to parents. Instead, we were shown onto an outside balcony running alongside the baby ward. It had triple-glazed windows, so no sound was heard from outside. Many of the babies we could see through the glass were in oxygen tents and, smiling, the nurse pointed to the small, oxygenized cot she had wheeled close to the window.

Our daughter lay in it, with thick black hair, just as Mike had said. She did seem a pretty baby, despite the tubes up her nose. She was no longer blue but a very pale pinky-white and she was sleeping peacefully on her side. As we watched, she stirred very slightly and puckered up her mouth as if she was dreaming; then she relaxed back into sleep. Still dressed up in overcoats and fur hats, for this was a chilly mid-April, we watched her together for some time and then Mike went to fetch Tauno. He stood shyly and somewhat awkwardly looking down through the window and then said: 'Sweet baby. Have you got a name for her?'

'Victoria,' I said. 'She's already been christened.'

He nodded but said nothing.

We went away. The whole experience had been strange, even dreamlike, almost nothing to do with us: one baby out of many, seen through thick glass, a nurse's baby.

Victoria. But we still didn't call her that when we mentioned her. Not yet.

For three weeks one of us would go to the hospital, taking the bottles of milk I had so eagerly expressed. It was the only thing I could do for her and I was sometimes frantic that there would not be enough or the milk would dry up before, just possibly, I might feed her myself. For about ten days we also looked at her daily through that glass window, until finally I was allowed into an ante-room to the ward, where a nurse brought her to me to hold for the very first time and to try to feed.

I took the bundle with the tiny pale face and the dark hair as if it were a cut-glass vase of priceless value that would shatter at a touch. I looked down at her and her eyes opened, bright eyes that looked straight into mine.

'Hello, little one,' I murmured.

We stared at each other. Did she, I wondered, have any feeling at all of knowing me, who I was? I didn't think it really possible but, despite that, I fancied that she did – or at least that I was somehow a familiar face from a long-distant past which she was struggling to place.

The nurse put her to my breast and her mouth nuzzled around, vainly searching. Then suddenly SNAP! But either one or both of us had not got the hang of it yet, for in a few seconds she unlatched herself. These attempts went on for some time, while I felt increasingly inadequate. The nurse said kindly: 'Never mind. We'll try again tomorrow.'

All the while, though, the very bright eyes had never left mine. For an instant I allowed myself to think: 'She seems OK to me. Could you look so searchingly and insistently if your brain was gone?' Then I closed my mind again, because hope was too dangerous.

Mike, of course, had not been allowed in, only 'the mother'. He had still not held her or seen that bright gaze. I described it as he squeezed my hand and I told him what I had thought at the time. Whether he believed me or not, I don't know, but probably he too thought hope was a dangerous thing. Mike had grown up in Calvinist Scotland, where in his generation you were brought up not to show your feelings, whether of sorrow or of joy, much like Finnish men were perhaps. 'Lack of communication' it would be called today, and I have always felt that for such men it was another type of handicap, an emotional one this time.

For the rest of the three weeks, even though the baby and I were getting reasonably successful at breast-feeding, we still made the daily milk deliveries, so that she would continue to get my milk at every feed. I had no idea whether there was any difference in the milk from different mothers, but I reasoned that perhaps there was a particular taste and smell which she would know again and it would help her to recognize me. She and Mike, however, had still to meet and remained completely unknown to each other, the view from the balcony being all that he was allowed.

One day, Pelle rang.

'She's doing well,' he said. 'You can take her home on Friday.'

CHAPTER 4

We were still quite unprepared. Although our child had been born and I had had time in the intervening three weeks before she was allowed home, superstitiously we had not dared to buy anything in the baby line. In case. However, in the corner of the little room, once Mike's study and now destined as a baby-room-cum-study – we were obviously first parents and naïve about babies – there was sitting a Finnish Maternity Box. The Finns, now as then, provide a box, a sort of starter kit, for all mothers-to-be as part of the health care system. Mothers can choose between the box and a sum of money, but most first-time mothers choose the box, which has a good reputation and is worth very much more than the money.

The box had arrived the previous month and we had examined its contents inquisitively.

'Nappies,' I said, pulling out the familiar towelling squares.

'Substitute ciggie,' said Mike, pulling something else out.

'What?' I asked.

'Substitute ciggie,' he repeated, showing me a dummy.

We had noticed that Finnish babies and young children mostly all had dummies. In England dummies were frowned upon as being bad for the development of baby's mouths as well as being 'lower class', and both were ideas which we later dismissed as utter nonsense.

'What on earth is this?' I held up a minute piece of flannel, cut in a way I had never seen before.

'No idea,' said Mike. 'Some sort of vest?'

We went through the rest – glass babies' bottles, bootees, a bib, a quilt, a shawl, a couple of hats, thick cotton leggings, a padded jacket, and lots of items we couldn't really identify. Most of the clothing was a genderless cream or yellow.

'Gosh!' I said. 'Everything is so tiny!'

Clearly, too, Finnish babies were dressed differently from British ones. Not that either of us had had any close acquaintance with babies in either country. I had never been a girlie-girl and played with dolls and prams, preferring the more adventurous boys' games, so I had not gravitated towards babies particularly. In Finland we singles had rather naturally socialized with other singles, as later when we were parents we mixed with other parents. I liked children but in a rather abstract way. My family in England had been extremely sceptical about my ability in any way to cope with a baby or small child.

Just as I had had no interest in dolls, so I had had no interest in the womanly skills of knitting or sewing, although I had been taught them, as girls always were. Other mothers, I knew, sewed and knitted wonderful layettes for their babies, with delicate, complicated patterns and could turn a heel or cast off fingers and thumbs with aplomb. My sole optimistic contribution had been a sleeveless vest which I had never finished off and one sleeve of an intended baby's cardigan. I still have them, and the vest is still unfinished.

I keep them as a salutary reminder of my failure to be an ideal mother.

However, now our baby was coming home. We got out the box and unpacked it again. The cardboard box, which was intended as a baby's crib, we put on the spare bed in the study, lined it with the small mattress provided and tucked round the sheets and blankets which had also been in the box. We never discussed buying a proper cot for our baby. Without saying it, we both knew that to buy one was like saying we knew she would survive and be all right.

When we fetched her from the hospital I put her into Mike's arms for the first time. He smiled down at her with gentle amusement, but I think his main feelings must have been ones of astonishment. Marrying late, he had never expected to have a child. He watched her as I clumsily changed her and cleaned her up at home. She squalled at the indignity – or perhaps sensed my lack of expertise – her face screwed up, little fists beating the air in random, uncontrolled movements, spaghetti legs rigid. In the bath, though, the wriggles were more of pleasure at the warm, womb-like liquid.

'She's like a little sprat,' said Mike.

From then on we called her the Sprat, which later developed into Spratty. At home she was never to be Victoria, the name I had given her while lying on that dark green slab and which we had not chosen together.

So Spratty continued to sleep in her cardboard box for many weeks. A 'three-months-colic' baby, she wailed unceasingly every evening from about 5.30 to 8.30 until I could stand it no longer and would walk out, abandoning my poor child. My mother, who had come from England to help me, had infinitely more patience than I had – or, I would like to think, was less emotionally taut and exhausted – and would sit for hours by her box, patting and stroking her, singing a lullaby over and over again until the wailing subsided into little sobs, then hiccups, and Spratty would finally fall asleep.

Although neither Mike nor I discussed our fears, we both watched her every reaction, every movement. We hung a mobile above her box and watched her eyes follow it.

'She can see, anyway.'

'Yes, she can obviously see.'

The telephone would ring and her head would turn.

'She can hear, can't she.'

'Yes and she reacts to our voices, too.'

She began to smile 'at the right time', to turn over, to sit up – it was all according to the Baby Bibles that we so anxiously read. I realized later that we were lucky that she did these things when the book said, as parents mostly learn later that the theory in books is one thing, the reality something else. Slowly our fears began to subside and almost, though not quite, to disappear: she was going to be all right – wasn't she?

We took the opportunity of my mother's visit to have her received into the Church of England. She had of course been baptized at birth by the Lutheran priest at the hospital, but we wanted to have an Anglican ceremony too. Our little church was allowed to use a chapel belonging to Helsinki Cathedral for its services, at which the regular churchgoers numbered about twenty-five to thirty. Despite this, its official title was the resounding English Chaplaincy of Helsinki, Moscow and Outer Mongolia – as the priest served all three places. Our own small congregation was scattered over a wide area round Helsinki and seldom met outside church services. Nevertheless it was a warm and friendly one – worshipping together in one's own language is very important and creates a strong bond – and the birth of a new baby was a fairly rare occasion for us all. Although some friends knew there had been trouble with Spratty's birth, at this age there was no sign of any disability. Throughout the ceremony her eyes flashed around with interest and she obliged the congregation with her best smiles. They simply rejoiced that the difficulty was now safely over and that she was forever theirs; a second-generation 'child of the church', which is how they would always think of her. We went happily back home for a party and almost forgot our faint worries.

An early trip to a children's specialist had also put us more at ease. Spratty's eyes had followed with interest the torch the doctor shone around the room and she had also responded to the various sounds of tuning forks at different pitches and at bells sounded at different noise levels behind and to the side of her ears. The doctor had examined her sitting up and lying down and pronounced everything to be quite normal – at least for the moment. We went away relieved, but still there was always that little niggle: 'Perfectly normal *for the moment.*' We continued to watch.

Spratty began to crawl very early, in a typically determined way. I had bought her the latest thing in babywear in England, a Babygro, an all-in-one stretch towelling suit with snap buttons from neck to one toe and in this she wriggled her way over the floor, faster and faster, like a small pink worm. She crawled by pulling herself along with her arms and pushing with her toes, right leg straight and left leg bent. I had read the books and knew that babies crawled in a variety of ways, some propelling themselves by their arms, some half on their bottoms and not necessarily in the traditional way of hands and knees.

She pulled herself up to stand; she took a few tentative steps – all if anything earlier than usual. She toddled as toddlers do, sturdy legs wide, staggering and losing her balance. If she very often fell – so what? So we were not worried, not then.

But as time went on and she continued to fall so often, we started to compare the others of her own age and younger. We saw, even if we didn't want to, that they walked better and fell seldom. We also noticed that when she kissed – and she loved kissing – she did not purse her lips but gave wet, puppy-dog kisses. Would not pursing her lips mean that she would have difficulty in speaking?

However, to our relief she began to say her first words very early and, as parents do with a first child, I noted them down carefully in a little book:

'More.'

'(M)ummy.'

'Wing-wing' – that was 'penguin', her favourite toy.

As for most parents and toddlers, her words were at first intelligible only to us – but they were words.

Then one day, she fell, bumped herself and began to cry. I bent down and comforted her, when suddenly she wriggled out of my arms and said: 'More cy no! More cy no!'

'Mike!' I called in excitement. 'Mike! She's said her first sentence!'

'What? What did she say?'

'"More cy no",' I repeated triumphantly. 'That's a sentence!'

He thought about it.

'Yes,' he said. 'I see. She means she won't cry any more, doesn't she.'

'Clever girl! Clever girl,' we both said together, cuddling her. Spratty looked smug.

In retrospect, what a significant and characteristic first sentence that was for the girl who bounced back optimistically from all life's bumps.

Spratty of course had the usual baby and toddler illnesses. Like all new parents, we were anxious about the smallest thing and the pages of Dr Spock's *Baby and Child Care*, the baby and toddler Bible of the period, were already dog-eared and falling to bits with our thumbing through such headings as Crying, Coughing, Bowel Movements,

Fever, Illness and so on. We would try not to call Pelle to ask what we should do but we inevitably did, and the always kind Pelle would often come over himself and see her, like the old-fashioned GP then rapidly becoming obsolete in Finland. On one such occasion, when she was about two, he said it was time for her to have a check-up with a specialist to see what effects the brain damage might have had, though it was still early days.

Our fears stirred again. What had he noticed? Was it more than the small things that had begun to bother us?

The specialist showed us into her room, which had brightly coloured toys and pictures everywhere. Spratty's eyes darted round with interest. She sat on my knee while the doctor tested her eyesight and hearing much as before and Spratty smiled gleefully, but when the funny lady shone lights into her eyes and peered through instruments, she wriggled and protested. It was better when she was asked to imitate the doctor and put differently shaped blocks of wood into the appropriate holes in a box. We had done this often at home and Spratty was very good at it.

'Good girl,' said the doctor approvingly and Spratty looked pleased. But the doctor turned to me and said: 'You see the way she holds them? You can see her co-ordination is a bit difficult.'

Could you? I hadn't noticed before.

'Now, Victoria, I'm going to show you some pictures. Can you tell me what this one is?' she said, showing her the picture of a cow.

'Caa,' said Spratty obligingly.

Next came a horse.

'Oss!' said Spratty. 'Oss!'

'Yes, it's a horse,' I said, interpreting.

We went through many others, all successfully, even if Spratty could not say 'h' or 's'. But that was typical of other toddlers of her age, surely?

'Now,' said the doctor, 'I'd like to see her walk across the room. Would you go to the door, please, and call her.'

I did so and Spratty came staggering over to me.

'Thank you,' said the doctor. 'Would you like to play with the box again, Victoria?'

So Spratty played on the floor with the box and the blocks while I went to sit in front of the doctor's desk.

'Well, Mrs Webster,' said the doctor. 'Victoria's case seems to be one of minimal cerebral palsy.'

Cerebral palsy. This was the first time the words had been said to us. I thought: 'Cerebral palsy – that's another phrase for spastic, isn't it? Isn't that the one where people shake? But Spratty doesn't do that. "Minimal" – minimal sounds encouraging.'

'Tell me,' said the doctor, 'was there difficulty at birth?'

I described what had happened.

'Yes,' she said, 'that would probably account for it. And nobody suggested a Caesarean?'

'No,' I said.

She pulled a face.

'About 80 per cent of cerebral palsy cases, you know, are caused by damage at birth or in the first month,' she said, 'and at least some could certainly be avoided by giving a Caesarean section.'

She paused, then went on sadly: 'As a specialist in the field I get somewhat frustrated when I see damage that could have been avoided.'

I knew all too well how she felt. I too wanted to blame the doctor who had delivered our baby, to be able to hate him, but it's so easy to blame and to hate. And who knows really in the end? It was done; it had happened. Could hate help that?

'I see you are expecting another baby,' she said. 'I hope you're going to have a Caesarean for that one.'

'Yes, yes,' I said. 'My doctor says there's no question.'

'Good,' she said. 'Now going back to your daughter – she has some spasticity and she's also probably slightly ataxic.'

What was ataxic? I should have asked but fear kept me silent.

'You are probably anxious to know the prognosis, though.'

Prognosis – another word I hadn't heard before but with which I was to become very familiar.

'Of course it's very early to tell much – and every case is different.'

'Will she be able to talk?' I asked.

'Probably. But her speech may not be clear. And she'll probably always speak slowly.'

'And walking?'

'We'll have to see. Perhaps she'll never be able to run. Her movements may be a bit clumsy and there may be a number of things she can't manage.'

'And school?'

'It's far too early to tell. She may be able to go to a normal school – you'll have to wait and see. There's a clinic for cerebral palsy cases here in Helsinki – Folkhälsan – it's Swedish-speaking, but I'm sure they will know English – and I should keep in touch with them. If you have problems with Victoria's speech or movement, they may be able to help you.'

We said good-bye and went back home. All the time the doctor and I had been talking, Spratty had been playing with the box, not listening to the grown-ups. Or was she? Later I wondered.

CHAPTER 5

When Mike returned from work, I told him the upshot of our visit to the specialist. Like me, he had seen the word 'Spastics' on the red-and-white collection boxes of the Spastics Society in Britain, had vaguely read the word occasionally in newspapers or magazines or had seen an advertisement of a child in a wheelchair with twisted spindly legs or claw-like hands. We looked up 'cerebral palsy' in a medical dictionary.

CEREBRAL PALSY can conveniently refer to the children with irremediable damage to the brain which, if it cannot get better, at least cannot get worse.

We looked down further to try to find the word 'ataxic' and came upon a list of up-to-now unfamiliar words:

HEMIPLEGIA: the paralysis of limbs on one side of the body.

QUADRIPLEGIA: the paralysis of all four limbs.

ATHETOID: in which voluntary movements are disturbed by involuntary ones.

'That's the one where your head and your limbs shake all over, isn't it?' I said. 'That must be Dr Johnson's one – they said he shook and made faces. And yet he was probably the greatest literary figure in eighteenth-century England. Imagine! That didn't stop him.'

And then, finally, there it was, the word we wanted.

ATAXIA; characterized by inco-ordination which includes lack of balance.

Beneath the list were the words:

The classification makes no use of the term 'spastic', which is simply the adjective employed for a special kind of disorder of the muscle which may or may not be present.

'Now there's a misused word – spastic,' commented Mike. 'People simply don't realize it means so little. I don't think I did either.'

But what we most wanted to know about was her mind. We read on:

75% of all cerebral palsy cases will have intelligence quotients in or below the educationally subnormal range.

So that meant that Spratty had a 25 per cent chance of having normal intelligence. It didn't seem a very good chance – but we didn't utter that thought out loud.

However, it is all too easy for a careless or over-confident doctor to dismiss as mentally defective a child with no manual abilities, no speech and uncontrollable facial movements. It has been stated before and it is worth stating again that 'the severity of the physical handicap is not necessarily related to the mental capacity'.

We thought about that too. Maybe as many as a quarter of those severely handicapped children who might not be able to do anything very much physically, but who nevertheless could think, could feel, trapped in a body that could not express itself. I remembered how helpless I had felt merely not being able to communicate in hospital in Finnish – how much more helpless these people must feel who had to face lack of communication every day. I wondered also how many of the 'village idiots' of the past – or even of the present in some parts of the world – were in reality perhaps simply athetoid or ataxic?

On the specialist's advice, we went to Folkhälsan. It was there that I saw other cerebral palsy children for the first time. I tried not to look too hard, but my eyes kept on being drawn towards them. I watched a father carrying in his son of about seven. The boy's legs were as thin as wires, one arm twisted and bent like a girder caught in a fire, his head crooked on one side. Another girl of about fourteen was in a wheelchair; shudders shook her head as if her chin was brushing flies from her shoulder and unintelligible stammers machine-gunned from her mouth. Only a year ago, I would have looked at them, kindly maybe, but supposing them also to be mentally impaired. But now I knew better: now I knew that as good an intelligence as anyone else, sensitivity, emotions could all lie locked in that crooked head, behind the machine-gun mouth, battering at some closed door to get out. I saw vividly how it might have been for Spratty and thanked God with profound gratitude that for her and us it had not been so.

The clinic confirmed her cerebral palsy.

'You should come back to us for a check-up every year. We'll see how she's getting on,' said the doctor.

'We thought perhaps she needs some physiotherapy,' said Mike.

'Yes, it would indeed be good. But you see,' the doctor looked apologetic, 'in your daughter's case the cerebral palsy is minimal. That's of course very lucky in one way, but we have to reserve the physiotherapy we can give for more severe cases. And there's such a shortage of physios here in Finland. There simply aren't enough to treat even all the severely affected children. It's the same with speech therapists – there aren't enough to go round. I'm so sorry.'

So were we; but having now seen some of the severe cases for ourselves, we realized that where it was a question of using resources where they were most needed, Spratty came very much at the bottom of the list.

'Can we do something ourselves then?' I asked.

'Yes, you could borrow some toys from our toy library,' said the doctor. 'They'll advise you there on some suitable ones for her age.'

'I didn't know such a thing existed,' I said.

'Well, if it weren't for voluntary contributions, it wouldn't,' said the doctor. 'But it's a way of helping parents who couldn't afford the special toys otherwise. Then there are ways you can help with her speech. I'll give you a list of exercises you could try with her.'

We went home and started at once on the exercises. Industriously we blew through straws into water, making delightful bubbles, and played games blowing ping-pong balls across the floor. All these games delighted Spratty for a while, until she became bored with being asked to play them every day and refused as adamantly as only a toddler can.

We searched for more help from books, but we could only find one on the subject – so little, it seemed, was known about it even by medical people. The one book, however, showed photographs of babies and toddlers with cerebral palsy which gut-churningly recalled Spratty: the open mouth with which she kissed, the arm-crawling, the legs stuck out like stabilizers when she sat. All these might have warned us earlier that she had cerebral palsy and, had we known earlier, we learned that we could have helped her more to develop her movements in a more normal way. For some things it was possibly too late. Again, it was nobody's fault. Pelle had not known about the possibility of helping babies in the early stages of developing movements any more than we had or anyone else, whether in the medical world or not. So we repressed the instinct to mourn the might-have-been, because now it was important to concentrate on the help we might be able to give her in the future.

By this time, I had had another child. My gynaecologist had advised us to have one as soon after the first as possible.

'But what if...?' we said.

'It's not likely to happen again,' she answered the unspoken question. 'You'll have a Caesarean next time and the baby will be fine.' She was the same gynaecologist who had looked after my previous pregnancy and who had been away at a conference when Spratty was born. Later she told me that she could never forgive herself for not being with me and, no matter how hard I tried to convince her that it was absolutely not her fault in any way, as it truly was not, she would not accept it.

I trusted her completely, however, and we followed her advice even if we were secretly afraid. I knew the statistics, too, about older parents being more likely to have a Downs Syndrome baby and I was scared of that possibility too. There were no advance tests for the condition then.

But all was well and, much to our surprise, I had a boy who, unlike Spratty, was given all ten points at birth. We still had no name for him, because our previous experience meant we did not dare count on his survival. Among the

Inuit and native American peoples, parents wait to give a name until they see what sort of character the child has – in their case, trying to detect which former ancestor has been reborn into the world. In our case we tried to see what name might suit him and, right up to the eve of the christening, had still not found an appropriate one. In despair we decided on a name – John – which was so common that it would do for all purposes and suit any character.

Spratty was enchanted with this new toy and showered him with kisses.

Before my second child I had already been back at work for eighteen months – maternity leave was three months then, but I had been fortunate enough to combine it with the summer vacation. Had I been living in England, I would certainly not have gone back to work after I had had my first baby, just as my Oxford contemporaries had not: general opinion plus the writings of child experts like Boulby were very much against mothers working when their children were young. In Finland, on the other hand, it was taken as the norm. Almost every mother I knew worked – indeed a second salary was needed to support the family. The result of this was that there was in place at least the beginnings of a system of child care which involved so-called 'park aunts' – women who would look after small children, some very young indeed, in the children's playgrounds which were to be found in every park, no matter how small. There were disadvantages to this, of course: it was always out of doors, which meant when the weather got very cold in the winter, the playground was closed, and it was only for a very few hours a day, so that parents had to make other arrangements for the rest of the day. There were some women who 'took in' a few children to be child-minded, just as there still are, but it was relatively unsupervised or not at all. Mike and I got by through a combination of park aunt, the annual visits of my mother, a home au pair during term-time and arranging our hours at the university to dovetail with each other so that mostly one of us could be at home if Spratty was ill.

We continued this system for some while after Johnny was born, but Spratty was growing out of park aunts and needed something more stimulating than the sandpit. The clinic had also advised us to try at all costs to get her into a 'normal' playschool and let her mix with non-handicapped children of her own age. We knew in advance that it was not going to be easy. Who was going to take a child with speech and movement problems? Wasn't it likely that they too, like most others, would equate physical handicap with mental handicap?

CHAPTER 6

We had decided to try and get her into a playschool run by Catholic nuns which was quite near the university and next to a beautiful park. Although the nuns were Dutch, the playschool was conducted in English, which we felt might make things a little bit easier for Spratty. We also thought that nuns were perhaps more likely to accept a handicapped child. I made an appointment to see them.

'Yes, we do still have a few places for the coming year,' said the Sister. 'How old is your child?'

'Four. Almost five,' I said.

She consulted her books. 'Yes,' she said. 'I think we could fit her in. And her name?'

'Victoria,' I said. 'But there is just one thing I think you ought to know – she is slightly spastic.'

'Oh,' said the Sister, trying to conceal her dismay.

'It's not very much. She's quite all right otherwise, you know.'

'Well,' said the Sister, 'I'm afraid that does make a difference, Mrs Webster. I hadn't realized there was any... Spastic, you said?'

Oh God, I thought, it's that word 'spastic'. It scares people; they associate it with deformity and mental problems.

'It's only that she walks clumsily – and her speech is a bit slow – but, she's bright – she's a bright child.'

The Sister was kind. 'The problem is, you see, that we don't have the time to… We have so many children. You know, I'm very sorry, but I'm afraid… the responsibility…'

I interrupted her before she could say it.

'Please,' I begged. 'Please. It's so important that she goes to an ordinary school. Let me bring her round. Then you can look at her and judge for yourself. Please.'

The Sister was reluctant but obviously also thought that she ought at least to see her. She told me to bring her round the following day.

I went home, at least a little optimistic. Spratty will win her round, I thought. I know she will.

Spratty had been a pretty baby and was growing into a pretty child. Her eyes were her most striking features – long-lashed, bright, merry and truthful. She could not lie, ever, because her eyes would betray her. She was so anxious to please, to be loved, that even the slightest verbal rebuke was enough to send her into sobs and endless 'sorries': 'Sorry, sorry Mummy, sorry…' until as parents we felt dreadful remorse and would hug her while she covered us with kisses. Her neat little nose was inherited from my mother, as was her perfect skin. Her mouth was also neat, but when under stress or worried or tired, one side of it would grow taut and get out of balance with the other. When she walked or ran – because indeed she could run despite the prognosis – one foot kicked out slightly to the side. She still fell easily, especially when tired, and then her speech would become more slurred as well. People noticed these things to begin with, but after spending time with her, they would forget them. That was what we hoped would happen at the playschool.

And it did. Although the Sister was still dubious, afraid of accidents and the responsibility, she agreed to take her on trial for two weeks – after that, they would have to see.

Joyfully, I returned to Mike.

'They're going to try her out for two weeks! So after that it will be all right – I know it will!'

For who could resist the small Victoria? Yes, she stumbled, but if she fell she would get up *herself* – nobody was to help her. She seldom cried about it unless she was really hurt. To begin with people found her speech hard to understand, but with time they did. She radiated confidence, optimism and joy, and she poured out love indiscriminately on babies, beetles, the old, a fly with one leg – anything and anyone which seemed to her to need her instant help. Few could not admire the patience and dogged determination with which she set out to master the skills of others of her age or her absolute conviction that there was nothing, ever, that she could not do. Faced with Everest, Spratty would climb it.

There were many Everests in her life even at this age: tying a shoelace, buttoning a coat, using a pair of scissors, blowing a whistle, skating... Bit by bit she taught herself the skills other children took for granted. It took her fifty or a hundred times longer than others of her own age, but in the end she did them.

Sometimes, though, it was not in quite the same way as the others. Skating was a particular problem for her because it demanded not only motor skills but also excellent balance. Finally, after endless afternoons on the ice, falling time and time again, she learned to propel herself round the rink with one foot at an angle of 40 degrees to the ice. This did not of course escape the critical eyes of other children. I would hear them say to their parents or each other: 'What's the matter with her?'

Or a child would speak to her: 'Why do you skate so funnily? What's the matter with you?'

'Nothing!' Spratty would answer indignantly. 'There's nothing the matter with me!'

I watched her continue with a mixture of love and compassion, anxiety and fear.

One evening, she said to me: 'Mummy, what's "spastic"?'

My stomach dived. 'Why do you ask, darling?'

'Well, at the ice-rink today a boy said that I was spastic.'

So the time had come, I thought. I wasn't going to avoid the question, which was bound to be asked sooner or later, but how do you explain cerebral palsy to a four-year-old who is without the technical vocabulary or maturity to understand? I did my best.

'You see, darling, you had a hard time being born. You had to push very hard to get out of me and your head got hurt.'

'How?' she asked with interest.

'Well, inside your head it's like – it's as if there were millions and millions of little wires – though they aren't real wires – and they send signals to your body about what it is to do. It's a bit like – well – electricity.'

'Erectricery?'

Spratty looked puzzled and I realized that of course she had no idea how electricity worked either. I tried again.

'It's sort of like little branches on a tree, all joined up. Well, when you were a baby, there was a piece that got broken, so the messages couldn't be sent in that part. For a long time we didn't know which part had got broken, but now we know it was a bit which tells your muscles how to move. And that's what doctors call being spastic. But most people don't understand what it means at all.'

Spratty said: 'But I can move my muscles, Mummy. I can.'

'Yes, but maybe not as quickly as other people.'

'But I *am* quick, Mummy!'

'Yes, I know you are, sweetie. But sometimes it takes you longer to do things than other children. Not **you**, but your muscles. You see, when the messages can't be sent through that bit in your brain, they have to be sent another way. Your brain has to learn to do that. Like a path coming to an end and you have to find another path to go along. And it might be a longer way, so it's slower. Do you see? You can't move your muscles quite as fast as you would otherwise – jumping's harder and so on.'

Spratty instantly started jumping up and down.

'But I *can* jump, Mummy! Look at me. I'm jumping. I'm good at jumping, aren't I?'

I supposed that I had explained badly it and that she didn't understand, but then I decided it wasn't that. She did know about herself deep down but she just wasn't going to accept that there was anything about her that would prevent her from being like other children. That was her strength: her refusal to believe that there was anything she could not master.

And that was how she continued. After a while, Mike and I became convinced that she was right, because that way her self-belief and dignity remained intact, qualities you desperately need if you have any kind of disability and the worse the disability, the more you need them. We never referred to the matter again until she was a teenager, when she brought it up herself.

It was later that year that we went to England on our annual visit and round of friends and relatives. We had read earlier about a Hungarian doctor who was a specialist in cerebral palsy children and who had a practice in London. It seemed a great chance to find out more, so we made an appointment to visit him and see what he thought about Spratty, and 'the prognosis', as we had now learned to call it – and what we should do to help her.

The specialist was waiting for us in his room, wearing a doctor's white coat. We went through the case history and he gave her the usual tests: picking up things, describing pictures, precision finger-movement testing and so on. Then he asked us to take her clothes off down to her knickers – she didn't like this – and watched her as she walked across the room and also balanced on a kind of large rubber tyre.

'Hm,' he said, watching. 'Yes, you can see her balance isn't normal. Can she stand on one leg?'

'I'm not sure.' I said. 'Can you stand on one leg, darling? Try!'

Spratty obligingly tried – and tried – but she couldn't do it.

'No, she can't do that, can she,' he said.

Spratty studied him.

He filled a cup of water and gave it to me.

'See if she can carry this over there,' he said.

'Look, darling,' I said to Spratty. 'Can you carry this cup of water over to Daddy?' She didn't move.

'Go on, darling,' I said. 'Daddy wants the water. Just give it to him.'

Spratty picked up the cup and started carrying it. It spilt. She put it on the table, where it spilt again.

'No, you notice she can't do that either, can she?' said the specialist.

At the end, Spratty sat silent on Mike's knee while the specialist spoke to us about her.

'She obviously has motor and co-ordination problems,' he said. 'There are a lot of things she can't do. Perhaps she may never be able to do them. We must see. Come back to me in a year's time and we will check her progress again.'

We went out with Spratty into the London street. She had been unusually silent during the session, because she mostly chatted amicably non-stop.

As we walked along, she said: 'Am I going to see that man again?'

'Yes, next year. When you're five,' said Mike.

'I don't want to,' she said.

'Why not?' he asked.

'He wasn't nice. He didn't speak to me. He only spoke to you and Mummy.'

True. He had looked over her head at us and spoken of 'she' and 'her' as if she had not been present. To him she was obviously just a case. He couldn't know very much about children, we thought, however much he knew in theory. Spratty's dignity had been deeply offended: she was there, she could understand, she was a person. Furthermore, although she didn't say so, we were perfectly sure that she had understood the gist of what the doctor was saying to us, which amounted to the belief that she could not do things other children did. To Spratty, she could, she would, she was not different at all.

She never forgot this visit and was to tell me as an adult: 'I hated it! He was both watching me and ignoring me. He didn't behave towards me like the other adults I loved and trusted, who thought I had a brain. I probably couldn't understand what he said, but I wanted to feel I did.'

When the time came for us to make the return appointment, Spratty absolutely refused to go and no amount of loving persuasion would make her. From that moment on, she refused to see *anyone* in a white coat, a state which was to last for over ten years. For decades after this, too, she was to measure her progress in co-ordination by whether she could carry a coffee cup across the room without spilling it.

CHAPTER 7

We had been surprised to meet such thoughtlessness on the part of the children's specialist, but we were by now experienced in the variety of ways in which adults reacted to Spratty's handicap.

My mother, who came out every year to stay with us in Finland, adored her. She loved both our children, but Spratty was 'special', which is a positive word as opposed to the potentially negative 'different'. However, just for the very reason that she adored her, there was an extra problem, because my mother wished at all costs to protect her. This meant that she was appalled when we let Spratty try to skate or ride a bicycle.

'But you can't!' she would protest with tears in her eyes. 'She'll fall. She may hurt herself.'

Sometimes Spratty would be allowed to go to the nearby shops to fetch some milk or buy sweets with her pocket money. She would be very proud to be entrusted with such a grown-up mission, but again my mother would protest: 'Oh darling, are you really going to let her go *alone*!'

It was the going alone that was so important to Spratty, because it showed we thought her perfectly capable of doing it and that we trusted her. In this she was no different from any other child, but it was extra important for her, as it proved she was 'like other children'. My mother's worries were not in those days because of potential kidnappers or paedophiles, as they might sadly be in Britain today, but that in some more unspecified way she might be hurt.

We would try vainly to explain that it was particularly important for Spratty to do what other children did and to feel she was like them.

'But she's not like other children,' my mother would say simply.

'Yes, but...' we would begin – but it was no good. We felt pulled in two ways: on the one hand because Mike and I wished profoundly to protect Spratty too. I would wonder sometimes if we were unnatural parents, uncaring about her getting hurt, although inside I would know that we were not – it was because we cared about her so much that we wanted to boost her confidence. Instinctively – or perhaps because of Spratty's character – we knew that the most important thing to do was *not* to treat her differently and not to make her feel different. On the other hand, I worried that we grieved my mother. But we knew that we had to continue to let Spratty do even potentially quite dangerous things. Occasionally acquaintances would express surprise that we allowed her to do them, but usually it was unspoken and only revealed by an expression on their faces, instantly controlled.

All our many friends, both in Finland and the UK, made no comment at all, treating Spratty as we did – as they would any friend's child. Nor did we discuss the subject with them. This was no doubt partly because we seldom met friends except when we were with our children and we would not discuss them then. We talked a great deal at work when we were with our colleagues, but seldom about our private lives. However, Mike's and my whole unspoken policy from the outset was not to make Spratty different, either in our outward lives or in our hearts. It was not that we were 'in denial', as the fashionable phrase has it, because it was an inescapable outward fact, but to make it uppermost in our considerations, as my mother did, would have paralysed us emotionally from letting her do everything that other children of her age did. No doubt friends and acquaintances discussed her among themselves, probably with affection and sorrow, but not with us.

When we went on our round of annual visits to our relations and friends in the UK, it was the same. Taking their cue from us, or from natural tact, they made no direct comment and asked no questions. So Spratty grew up with a solid background of support, encouragement and love from those close to her. Indeed, it could be truly said that to us as a family she was not different at all. She was simply and uniquely Spratty.

That is, she was unless an event or something said would remind us that this was not true for the outside world. There were the strangers, those we passed in the street or met in the park or saw in shops both in Finland and in England. To begin with, when she was a baby or a toddler, nobody noticed. If she fell a lot, was unsteady on her feet, clumsy with her movements, or hard to understand, well, she was just a toddler and that was completely normal. By her mid-threes, however, people began to realize that 'something was wrong'. One could see by the covert looks of the adults and the open stares of the children. We became used to the all-pervading assumption that physical handicap meant mental handicap. Instead of asking Spratty the standard adult-to-child openers of 'What's your name?' and 'How old are you?', they would turn to us and ask 'What's her name?' or 'How old is she?', to which we would react by turning pointedly to Spratty herself and saying 'Go on, darling, tell her how old you are.' Why do people do it? Mere politeness would suggest speaking to the person concerned if they are present, whether child or adult. Are they afraid of embarrassing the parents? Are they afraid of being embarrassed themselves? Are they simply afraid?

If strangers or even acquaintances spoke to her, it would be slowly and loudly, as in the classic cliché of how people speak to a foreigner who doesn't know their language. It never seemed to occur to them that Spratty could understand as much as – and indeed sometimes more than – anyone else of her age. When she was of school age, the questions were rather different, like the time Spratty returned from a shop and said: 'Mummy, they asked me in the shop whether I went to a special school. Why did they ask me that? I'm not ill, am I, Mummy?'

'No, of course you aren't ill, darling,' I said. 'There's no reason at all for you to be in a special school.'

And there wasn't. But that was what people always asked, though with friends and relatives it took more tactful forms: 'What school do you go to?' 'Does your brother go to the same school?' We all understood perfectly well what was meant: blurred speech equals a blurred mind.

Reactions to Spratty became for us and later for her too a kind of test of people: how long would it take for the penny to drop that she had no mental handicap and was in fact very intelligent? There were and are those who never seemed to realize; there were those who would pick up the clues we would sometimes drop and whose attitude magically changed; and there were those few, thank God, who from the outset never treated her in any way differently from others. We would often discover later that such people had past experience of those with handicaps, either within their own family or a friend's family, or whose work had made them beware of assumptions about abilities.

If we had been in some other countries or places, there would have been much more to bear: the assumption that a handicapped child is the result of some fault or sin of the parents. A Finnish friend of mine who works with badly sight-impaired children in the Middle East and Asian countries tells me with sadness that the problems, difficulties and sufferings for both child and parent are often compounded by the fact that in many communities she visits it is assumed that the handicap is a punishment for wrong-doing. So both parents and child may be ostracized, bullied or even expelled from the community for perceived sin.

This attitude had not been totally eradicated in the western world either. The book we had read earlier had warned:

Many people in the community have quite wrong ideas about the reason children are born handicapped. There is an immediate thought: 'Is it due to wrong past behaviour? Is there alcoholism or any taint in the family?' This attitude to handicapped children clouds the picture even today.

And that attitude lingers on even now, sometimes without people being really conscious of it. How many ask about this and other perceived 'disasters': 'What have I/we/they done to deserve it?' as if life were a series of rewards and punishments? It is certainly true that some children's quality of life may be affected through the bad habits of their parents, such as smoking or alcohol or drug abuse, but the cancers or deformities caused by nuclear or chemical pollution, for instance, can hardly be blamed on the victims.

This attitude is very old. One of the stories about Jesus says:

He saw a man who was blind from birth. And his disciples asked him: 'Who sinned – this man or his parents – that he was born blind?' Jesus answered: 'This man has not sinned, nor have his parents.'

Some still ask that same question over 2,000 years later.

People also tend to forget entirely that there are unseen handicaps – or perhaps a more accurate word is deformities – of character of a much more malignant nature, such as malice and cruelty. These, though not visible and immediately recognizable, are able not only to impair the life of that person but, much worse, they find their outlet in deforming the lives of others.

It is also a common mistake for outsiders to assume that parents necessarily see a handicapped child or relative as a burden. No doubt some do and nobody should blame them. At the beginning I had assumed I would see her as one myself – I had prayed that God would send me the strength to 'bear this burden'. My prayers had indeed been answered, yet not in the basic yes/no way I had expected – as prayers often are not – for the simple answer had been that from the moment she came home after her birth, I never considered her as a burden in any way. And I am sure that if the parents who have cared for even a severely handicapped child at home were asked whether they would rather have gone through life without that child, the answer would usually be 'No!' This also applies to those with mental handicaps. I have, for instance, met the families of Downs Syndrome children who have spoken of it as a blessing and of what it has meant to them all, including siblings, in the development of their own understanding of others, their sensitivity and mutual love.

I can only speak for myself, although I believe I speak too for the rest of my family and friends: as far as Spratty's minimal handicap goes, it has from the moment she came home after birth been a source of a profounder understanding of many things and of a greater sympathy for others who are the object of discrimination of any kind. Life would definitely have been the poorer without her.

CHAPTER *8*

By now Spratty was almost six and it was time to start thinking about Big School. This had been a moment we were dreading, when she would be outside the sphere in which we could to some extent protect her; when she would be faced by the curious eyes, the non-understanding and the unthinking cruelty of society. For Spratty, of course, the thought was just as exciting as it would be for any other child – when at one step your status changes from 'little one' to the much more grown-up category of 'schoolboy' or 'schoolgirl'.

For hours we debated which school it should be. We were not going to consider any kind of special school as not only was it essential for her psychological development that she was in a school like any other but we also knew her to be an able child, even if – we remembered the prognoses – she turned out to be poor at some things, like maths or music.

She had already learned to read, as we had begun at home. The Finnish educational authorities frowned on teaching children to read before they began school, but it seemed to us wrong to prevent a child if she was as eager to read as Spratty was. So we imported the *Janet and John* series of books from England, where they were universally used in teaching millions of children to read. Together with Mike's or my pointing finger, we progressed from Book 1a

This is Janet.
This is John.
Come, John, come.
Look, John, look.

Through books 1b, 2a, 2b, 3a, 3b to 4a:

Mother went to a shop.
'I want a cap,' she said.
'I want a cap for John.'
She saw a brown cap. She saw a blue cap.
'I like the blue cap,' she said.

We also used a small child-sized work called *Ant and Bee,* which was brilliant for early reading but which was so popular with Spratty (and later Johnny) that we could no longer bear to hear the simple saga over and over again and hid it on top of a cupboard.

So we knew Spratty was a quick and eager learner and would manage school. But which school? And school in Finland or England?

England we dismissed from the outset. It meant boarding school. We had friends from the British Embassy who sent their children (especially their sons) off to boarding school in England at the age of seven, but to us it seemed an inhuman system, a hang-over from the days of the British Empire when parents had been posted to distant places where there were no schools or the climate was unhealthy. It is also a class system, or at least one that requires the parents to have the money to pay the usually very high fees. We realized that older children might actually find the idea attractive and some possibly thrive better outside their own family environment; but we decided that a seven-year-old needs parenting, needs home love, comfort and support, and teachers in a boarding school cannot possibly have as much time to give to every child as a parent does. Today the situation is even worse, as teachers in Britain are prevented from giving physical expressions of comfort and affection to children of any age in case it is construed as sexual harassment – even an arm round a shoulder has been interpreted in this way. However, even if we had for a moment considered sending Spratty away to England, we were aware that she had more need than most for daily support from home.

She had of course another handicap when it came to school in Finland: she didn't speak either of the native languages. So we investigated English-speaking schools first.

'There's the British School here,' said Mike.

'Mm,' I said, 'but I think that only takes them till they're eleven. Then they assume the children will go off to school in their own countries – or before, because a lot of the parents are diplomats.'

'Then that means boarding school later. So no good,' said Mike.

'There's a school called the English School too,' I said. 'Run by nuns – but not English ones, I think, and I'm not sure how much they do in English either.'

'Anyway,' I said, 'a Finnish school would probably be better – she'd have Finnish friends. That's important if we're staying on here.'

Mike glanced at me. For a while before Spratty was born, we had considered moving on and taking up a British Council post we had been offered in Nigeria. The birth of

Spratty had changed that; we did not know what would happen but we felt we needed to be near good medical help and advice which, rightly or wrongly, we did not think we would get as easily in Lagos.

'Yes,' he agreed. 'If she went to a school with other foreign children, they would be bound to up and leave at some point and she would lose her friends.'

I nodded. 'Friends are very important.'

'A Finnish-speaking school then,' I said.

'Or a Swedish-speaking one, of course,' said Mike.

Finland is a bilingual country like Belgium, with the majority of the population speaking Finnish and a decreasing minority speaking Swedish. The first consideration in the choice of a school by parents is therefore the language. It didn't really matter to us of course, so we started looking round for Finnish schools in general, not all that enthusiastically. The lack of enthusiasm was because education in Finland at that time was based very much on the old German system. It was very much teacher-centred and concentrated on memorizing and regurgitating what you had been taught, which was mostly facts. There was little encouragement for the pupils to think and reason for themselves or to question. Language teaching centred on translation and writing, not speech, and no foreign literature was taught at all. Mike and I encountered the end product at university and tried valiantly but mostly in vain not only to make our students talk, even if they made mistakes, but above all to make them question what we said and write their own opinions rather than those of others. It was a struggle. Things were to change very much from the next decade onwards, but not yet.

Then by chance we were invited round to have tea with Anneli, an ex-student of ours. After university, she had gone off to Germany to train to be a Steiner school teacher and had now returned to Finland.

At tea Anneli spoke enthusiastically about the Steiner school and showed us some of the workbooks her pupils produced. She also told us of the amount of drama the pupils did, the art and music and the work experience they all did later. She produced examples, too, of the project work which every pupil did on their own. It all sounded to us a stimulating system which encouraged individuality and independent thought.

'Have you thought about putting Spratty in the Steiner school?' asked Anneli.

'But isn't it a private school?' I asked.

'Not in the English sense of private schools,' said Anneli. 'All kinds of children go. The parents aren't all well-off people – they come from very different backgrounds, but they are all people who believe in this type of education.'

'But it does have fees,' said Mike.

'Yes,' said Anneli. 'But they aren't very high.' She mentioned a sum which seemed to us derisory compared with what the fees would be at an English private school.

'It's Finnish-speaking, isn't it?' I said.

'It's both,' said Anneli. 'In fact it's the only school in Finland which has parallel classes, one in Finnish, one in Swedish.'

'Then that would mean that an English-speaking child would not stand out so much,' I said. 'I mean the other pupils would understand that children spoke other languages. Young children don't always realize that. An Anglo-Finnish child I knew thought that children always spoke Finnish and grown-ups spoke English, for instance.'

'Why don't you come and see the school for yourselves?' said Anneli. 'I'll show you round.'

It was a fairly new school, light and airy and decorated with watercolours of the kind we would later call 'Steineresque' – soft, flowing mixtures of pale pinks, yellow, lilac and greens. It was also set in pleasant surroundings, off the main road and at the edge of the forested Central Park, since the Steiner theory believes in surrounding children as much as possible with the beauties of nature. We learned more things that attracted us. Here the pupils were not pressurized into staying on until eighteen or nineteen and taking their Matriculation exams, roughly the equivalent of A-levels, as happened in other Finnish schools. The school encouraged pupils to discover what they wanted to do in life and then to act accordingly – staying on if they had an academic turn of mind or wanted to do something that required the exam or a degree; leaving school at sixteen and taking other training if you wanted to be, say, a gardener or an artist. Both Mike and I happened to have been to university ourselves (for neither of us had it been a foregone conclusion), but we both firmly believed our children did not have to follow that path unless they wished. Spratty was to say later that one of the things she was very grateful to the Steiner school for was that it believed in following your dreams – which was exactly what she did.

The school also allowed children to develop skills at their own speed. There was no pressure, for instance, on a child to read by the end of the first year – or even the second. At a parents' meeting, the mother of a boy of nine was extremely worried that her son could still not read.

'Don't worry,' said the teacher. 'We have never had a child who couldn't read in the end.'

Sure enough, by the end of that year, the boy could read.

In many a school system these days such a boy would cause great concern, go to special classes or even a special school, feel ashamed or stupid and might be stigmatized by his classmates, if not others, as 'backward', 'a dummy' and so on. His whole future life might be affected. Yet it is surely totally obvious to anybody who has much to do with young children that they do learn skills at different rates. If as parents we go to a clinic worried that our toddler cannot walk or talk at the so-called normal age we are assured of this, so why are we not assured in the same way when our children go to school? I learned to read when I was four – I was certainly not a phenomenon, just a second child who saw her sister reading. The highly intelligent daughter of a friend could not read until she was ten – although, oddly enough, she could write. Of course, the inability to read at 'the right age' can be the sign of something wrong, but it does not necessarily mean this. It is simply another common assumption.

We did hear some other of Rudolf Steiner's theories which we thought strange or even ridiculous. We were not those who believed, for instance, that all of us had coloured auras round us which some special people could actually see. But the school did not press this or other Steiner theories on either parents or children.

'And if the school does the right things for reasons we don't agree with,' said Mike, 'does it really matter?'

So the Steiner school seemed the right school for us. Perhaps also we had heard that Steiner schools were reputed to take on difficult or unusual children and felt that Spratty would therefore be more acceptable to them, but if so, it was not a prime reason.

The Steiner school accepted her without question after an interview. They had had one suggestion to make, though: we had assumed she would go into the Finnish-speaking class, but the school suggested the Swedish-speaking one would be better for her.

'In the Finnish-speaking classes, you see,' said the teacher, 'the children learn German as their first foreign language, but they begin with English in the Swedish-speaking ones, so that would make it easier for her.'

'When do they start a language?' I asked.

'Right at the beginning – in the first class. It's done through rhymes and songs at that stage, of course, but we do start right away.'

Again I was surprised: a foreign language – as opposed to the second national language – was not started that early in other Finnish schools. But it was a good age to begin, I thought, since young children were brilliant imitators.

'But she would learn Finnish too in the Swedish-speaking class, I suppose, ' said Mike.

'Yes,' said the teacher. 'And of course Swedish in the Finnish-speaking class.'

'When do they start English in that one?' he asked.

'Not until later – at twelve. And the Swedish class does German then.'

'I see. So either way she'll end up with four languages.'

'Yes, but in the Swedish-class she'll only start with two instead of three, as she already knows English.'

We thought about it. Yes, the Swedish speaking class would be the sensible one to put her in. It would give Spratty an advantage at the start when it came to English lessons at least and an advantage was what she needed. It was just that...

'She knows a little Finnish from the local children,' I said. 'But she doesn't know a word of Swedish.'

'She'll catch up,' said the teacher confidently. 'At the end of the year she'll be speaking Swedish just like the rest. You'll see.'

We were deeply pleased that the teacher had the perception to see that Spratty would manage as well as any other child and decided that the advice about the class was good.

When it became her brother Johnny's turn to go to school, we did the same for the same reasons. As it turned out, the school's advice and our decision was to be a crucial factor in Spratty's later career and, to some extent, also in

Johnny's. They grew up trilingual, a gift for the future as effective as any fairy godmother's.

So Spratty went to the Steiner school's pre-school class at the age of six – another way in which it was ahead of its time, since pre-school classes were almost unknown then.

As I wrote in that year's Christmas letter: 'Spratty adores it (not that she wouldn't adore any school – she's one of the world's born schoolgirls).'

So all seemed well. But of course this was pre-school: Big School lay ahead and Big School turned out to be a different Everest.

CHAPTER 9

So here we had a child with cerebral palsy who was beginning school not only in one foreign language but a second. We had certainly not made things easier for her in that way, however much we believed she could cope. Had we done right? We really did not know.

In addition, although things had gone well in the pre-school class, our fears began to focus on how she would be treated – not by her class teacher, who was so obviously kind and caring, but by her classmates. I knew how young children reacted to those with even the slightest physical difference from their own norm. I had had to wear glasses from the age of nine and I knew the teasing 'Four eyes! Four eyes!' or later as a teenager the repetition of the rhyme:

Men never make passes
At girls who wear glasses.

This was a rhyme which I had seriously believed to be true for very many years and which had led to many an embarrassing situation, since I would take off my glasses at dances or parties. As I was very shortsighted, this would lead me to asking friends desperately: 'Who's that over there?', to cutting people or smiling broadly at strangers, and quite often to walking into the Gents instead of the Ladies. I never went as far as an even more shortsighted cousin of mine, though, who once, when taking a letter to post in one of the old round red pillar-boxes, tried to post it in a woman with a red coat.

Other unfortunate children were singled out for having red hair, wearing braces on their teeth, lisping or stammering and so on. They still are. Added to that these days are those with racial or religious differences – worse prejudices no doubt but involving the same type of discrimination, jeering and bullying that so often attaches to 'the different'. Why is it? There are probably many reasons, but I sometimes suspect it could spring from a very primitive form of species survival: to cast out those with a perceived difference from the pack so that the species continues or the weakest do not hold up the rest.

As they grow up, most people – but not all – acquire other behaviour patterns and accept their correctness either genuinely or at least outwardly. Young children, however, most of whom are quite naturally self-centred and have not yet had time to develop much understanding of the feelings of others, tend to have a pack instinct which excludes the outsider. The make-up of the pack can also vary from day to day – one day a child is part of it, the next day not. If a child sides with the outsider, he or she is excluded too, and it is an unusual child who can stand the pressure of being excluded for the sake of another. A class is a pack and packs have leaders; the ethos of the pack – what the Steiner school calls 'the class spirit' – depends on the ethos of the leader or leaders. Any teacher, even of adults, will have experience of this and knows the mystery of parallel classes, taught the same things in the same way and having people in them of roughly the same intelligence, yet having totally different 'spirits'. I suspect that the amount, nature and type of bullying depends on this too.

In the Steiner system, each class has the same teacher from the age of seven until thirteen, when the class changes to one which has various subject teachers and one class supervisor. Spratty, though lucky in her sympathetic and experienced class teacher, was unlucky in her pack leaders and the class spirit was never good. Her brother Johnny, however, when it came to his turn, was lucky to have a class with a wonderful class spirit, many of his classmates becoming life-long friends. It was not so for Spratty – our fears were justified and she was frequently excluded from the pack and bullied.

This did not seem to be so at first. We believed that all was going well. There were frequent parents' meetings (another Steiner characteristic) and her teacher assured us that Spratty had no real problems: she was even quite good at maths. When it came to gym and the Steiner speciality of Eurhythmics – which reminded us of Greek dancing – where balance is important, she naturally had problems, but as her report said: '…her persistence and determination are amazing and a lesson to us all. She just won't give up.'

This was hardly a surprise to Mike and me. You could say that astonishment at her persistence was to be a characteristic reaction throughout her life from those who did not know her well.

Then one day I became conscious that she might be being bullied – although 'teasing' was what we called it then. I had taken her to school and walked as far as the school playground, which she had to cross to get to the school entrance. A smaller boy following her began to mimic her slight camel-like kick with one foot as she walked and another boy with him laughed and giggled. My usually suppressed emotions suddenly welled up and

I started to rush across the playground towards the boy. I wanted to shake him and to scream: 'Stop it! Stop it! What if you were her? How would you like to be mimicked and laughed at?'

But I stopped in time, controlled myself and thought: 'I mustn't interfere – it'll only make it worse for her when I'm not here to defend her.'

Yet it made me realize that all might not be well for Spratty and that she might be being teased without our knowing it. She had never spoken of it at home and had always been her own happy self when we picked her up, but we knew that children are often secretive about their school lives and that a typical parent–child conversation goes:

'Well, how was school today?'

'Boring.'

'What did you do?'

'Nothing.'

Children seem to compartmentalize their lives, and school is their own world, for good or bad uninfluenced by home and where home rules do not apply. Instead it is the school rules which apply, coupled – perhaps even more importantly – with the rules devised by their peers, rules which may sometimes be quite unknown to their teachers and intended to be so. But one rule is well known: at school you don't 'tell tales'; if you do, you will hear the rhyme:

Tell-tale-tit!
Your tongue shall be bit
And all the little puppy dogs shall have a little bit!

It was not just for this reason that Spratty did not speak about the bullying, we discovered. She was to explain later that when she came home, everything was different: the language, the meals, the pictures on the walls, the customs, everything. It was a different world, a refuge in which she felt safe and happy, where she could leave school and the outside world behind. The moment she spoke English with one of the family she was home.

After the incident with the mimicking boy in the school playground, though, I did tackle the subject with her at home:

'Spratty, do you get teased a lot at school?'

'Quite a lot.'

'What happens?'

'The boys kick me... or trip me up... or call me a spastic.'

I swallowed and asked carefully: 'Do you mind?'

Spratty considered the question.

'Well, Mummy,' she said, 'those who like me don't do it. So I don't mind the others so much. And then I know I'll be happy when I get home. So it's all right, Mummy.'

'So it's all right, Mummy.' I wondered where she got such wisdom, such tolerance. It would break another person. It would break me. If she could stand it, I thought, so must we.

Anybody today would ask: 'But didn't you say anything to the teachers?' A fair question, and the answer is 'No, we didn't.' We were afraid of making the situation worse by having Spratty labelled as a tell-tale as well as everything else and no doubt we thought that if she was still cheerful about it and quite happy to go to school every day, then it could not be too bad. It is also important to remember that twenty or thirty years ago 'bullying and harassment' had not become a general topic and a real issue. There was an attitude of 'Well, children will be children – they all tease each other at some point, over something'. 'Teasing'is a word that conveys a sense of not being very serious or even simply lightly joking. It is in the last sense a very

English characteristic, so much so that in England teasing can be a first sign of liking or even love. Teasing in the sense of persecution had as yet no public name in those days; the only other word available was 'bullying', which conveyed at the time the idea of purely physical abuse. The concept of verbal or psychological bullying had as yet not been publicly expressed, just as the common term of today 'harassment' and its offshoot 'sexual harassment' had not. If you have no name for something, it can seem as if it does not exist.

It was not her whole class who bullied and excluded her, simply a few individuals, unfortunately the leaders. They were both boys and girls – in fact, the girls often began it. Many of the pupils were swept along passively, although there were those who remained silent and were even friendly. Two called Tina and Eva were the closest she got to good friends, but there were others who did not join in and were even bullied as well: one boy who was rather small for his age and a couple of other girls. One of these Spratty said was bullied because she was 'not hard' and was considered too arty. As an adult, Spratty quoted something she had read on the subject: 'Teasing is the perception of the one teased.' She added: 'They may not have meant to be so cruel.' Twenty years later, at a class reunion, a man gave her an explanation from his point of view, although not a direct apology.

'I didn't want to go to the Steiner school,' he said. 'I wanted to go to the same schools as my friends – normal schools, not an abnormal school. And then you were in my class, and you were abnormal, so I was in an abnormal class in an abnormal school.'

And so he had bullied her. He seemed to think that this was a good enough reason. Spratty thought wryly that this explanation was really more revealing of himself as a person than of anything else.

However, at the same class meeting, another one of her male classmates came up to her to apologize for their behaviour to her when they were at school. He had tears in his eyes.

CHAPTER 10

Later, many people asked me, as I have also asked myself: what about the teachers – did they do nothing to stop the bullying? I suspect that the teachers knew little or nothing about it, because neither she nor I can believe that her caring main teacher would not have tried to stop it had she known. The tripping-up – all too easy with someone whose balance was not perfect – the kicking, the taking of her books, the hiding of her drawings, all went on covertly. Spratty describes a game her schoolmates used to play which they called Victoria-in-the-Cage. The game was for her classmates to put her in the middle and circle her with their desks. Gradually they pushed the desks closer and closer together and moved forwards, so that eventually she was forced to crawl under them to escape while they laughed and jeered at her. But this, she says, obviously never happened when a teacher was around and nor did a lot of the other bullying. Certainly at no time did the teacher speak to the class about bullying in general nor was the subject raised at any of the parents' meetings that we went to. Nor, it has to be admitted, did we raise it. Perhaps the teachers noticed some things but thought, as we did, that they might make matters worse if they drew attention to them.

I think now that matters cannot be made worse by talking about bullying and that we should have gone to the teachers, told them what we knew and talked it over with them. We should have done so right at the very beginning – or at least when we first realized it was going on. Children always test boundaries. The popular TV series where a professional nanny goes into a home to deal with the children's bad behaviour shows clearly that when she lays down the rules and then keeps to them exactly, the children's behaviour swiftly improves; the moment she leaves, the children start to test the parents on the rules and, the moment they relax them, the bad behaviour escalates in proportion. Parents at home know that the request for a glass of water at bedtime soon becomes yet another glass; throwing toys in anger becomes hitting siblings or parents; bullies who are allowed to bully will up the type and frequency of the bullying. Nor is testing boundaries confined to the world of children – it exists in the adult world and even internationally: a small-scale incursion into another country's territory, if nobody objects or intervenes, often becomes a full-scale occupation. It is the same with bullying: it must be stopped at the outset or more and worse will follow. I still blame myself today for not having done more to help prevent the bullying of Spratty.

Yet, despite everything, Spratty was happy at school. Little by little, step by step she overcame the potential learning hurdles. We had read about them:

Cerebral palsy children often have difficulties in perception. This may at school age make reading hard or even impossible.

We had already seen that one overcome.

Some cerebral palsied children may never have the ability to write. Others may write, but very slowly and illegibly.

She learned to write, not as neatly as some, but no worse than many.

A child with cerebral palsy may not be able to think logically; quite minor brain damage can impair memory and judgement and the estimation of probabilities may be impaired.

Her logic was one of her strengths; she delighted in solving problems and her memory was better than average.

Such a child may have difficulty in distinguishing sounds; he may not be able to close his eyes, blow, suck or wink. Individual finer movements may be hard or impossible.

Her hearing of sound was excellent, but her breath control was poor and her finger movements slower and more difficult to co-ordinate than for others. However, in the end, determination enabled her to manage to play the recorder, if not well.

And at the end of her third year at school, her Steiner-type report reads:

Victoria has continued to devote herself to school work with great enthusiasm. She has an obvious gift for words, which is shown in the ease with which she reads and understands the content of a text. Moreover she has experienced no difficulty in copying and has shown a marked interest in composition. Despite the fact that her classmates are at times a little surprised at Victoria's utter conviction that she can manage even the most demanding tasks, they are impressed by her courageous attitude to what confronts her at school. If Victoria does not succeed at something, she accepts it good-humouredly and tries again. In this respect she is a lesson to us all.

It is quite evident from this that she had an understanding and sympathetic class teacher and that she enjoyed school. But of course to Spratty the most important thing was the attitude to her of the other children. She wanted so desperately not just to be accepted by them but more than that: she remembers that more than anything she wanted to be considered one of the most popular and the most intelligent girls. It was never to be, although gradually even one or two of the boys did begin to half accept her as a person. One day she came home and said: 'You know, I think that perhaps Martin and Peter like me, Mummy.'

'What makes you think so?' I asked.

'Well, they don't want to show it, but when they kick me, they don't kick me hard, if you know what I mean, Mummy.'

And one day a thousand volts and Spratty burst into the house with: 'Guess what, Mummy! We had our Christmas party, and do you know what? Peter danced with me, Mummy. He danced with *me*! Do you know what, Mummy? I know one person who's not going to call me spastic from now on – or not meaning it, anyway. Don't you think so, Mummy?'

I hugged her tight, not finding any words.

Of course the bullying did not stop after that, but at least we all knew that Spratty was not entirely without support in her world. However, she still lacked what she so ardently desired – a Best Friend. All children crave friends and Spratty probably craved them more than most. Much earlier on, in a Christmas letter to my family in England when she was six and Johnny was four, I had described the different characters of our two children. This was the one in which I had said that Spratty was one of the world's born schoolgirls and had gone on:

Johnny is not one of the world's born schoolboys and only goes to playschool reluctantly. We notice, however, that he is very popular, mainly because he refuses to make overtures and has a lot of verbal wit – when he cares to speak. Spratty, on the other hand, who wants more than anything to be loved by everybody and who makes all the overtures, constantly suffers rejection – when the boys play cowboys and Indians it is she who is always the prisoner. Such is life. For those of you who don't know her, she has the sweetest nature – loving, kind and always thoughtful of others. Her tears already flow for the poor and the hurt and the ill in the world.

'The child is father of the man,' wrote the poet Wordsworth. Yes and the mother of the woman too.

Although at school she was never to have a special friend, she did have friends of her own age back where we lived. They were a group of six or seven boys (including Johnny) plus Spratty who were growing up together and who played in the communal garden. These were the boys I was referring to in the letter about the cowboy and Indian games. They had known Spratty as toddlers and they all accepted her without question and without bullying her in any way. She was a part of their lives. True, she was always the prisoner and, when they played ice-hockey, she always had to be the goal-keeper; but she was good at goal-keeping, where falling on the puck can be an advantage as well as is throwing yourself full length across the mouth of the goal. As she said: 'I spent more time horizontally than vertically when on ice anyway!'

So the boys found her useful and she was delighted to be of use. It also meant that she grew up with an unusual understanding and familiarity with boys which in the gender grouping that goes on among young schoolchildren was fairly uncommon. These boys could be said to have balanced out the impression made on her by the bullying boys (and girls) at school. Later, she was always to find herself at ease with men.

One day she came home and told us they had been talking at school about what they wanted to do when they grew up.

'Eva and Tina say they're going to be gardeners,' she said, 'and Veronica's going to be an artist of course and Annette's going to do jewellery like her father.'

'And what did you say?' asked Mike.

'Oh, I'm going to be a doctor,' said Spratty.

'Are you?' I said in surprise, perhaps remembering her aversion to people in white coats.

'Yes,' she said simply. 'The others said I couldn't be. But I am.'

'Well,' I said, 'a doctor in the family would be very useful.'

Afterwards, though, I said to Mike: 'Oh dear, I hope she hasn't set her heart on it. I'm afraid that's one thing that would prove impossible – even for her.'

'Oh, don't worry,' he said. 'She's only eleven. She'll change her mind several times before she's grown up.'

We really should have known better.

CHAPTER 11

At thirteen Spratty and the others moved up into the first of the classes in secondary school. I had always supposed that as the children grew up and became more educated and adult they would also become more tolerant and understanding of Spratty's handicap, so that life at school would be that much easier for her. It did not work out quite like that.

Spratty never spoke about being teased these days and we assumed it had been a bad period that was over. However, one day the telephone rang at home.

'Can I speak to Victoria?' said a young voice in Swedish.

'Yes, just a minute,' I said.

'Spratty!' I called. 'It's for you.'

'Who is it?' she asked.

'Don't know,' I said. 'Sounded like a friend from school.'

Spratty ran to the phone, excited by the idea that a schoolmate was actually phoning her.

I heard her answer, listen, and then saw her face change from one of happy expectation to one of shock.

'Who's speaking?' she asked in almost a whisper.

Whoever it was obviously hung up and Spratty put down the phone slowly and then burst into tears.

'What is it, darling?' I asked and rushed to put my arms round her. 'Who was it? What did they say?'

She couldn't speak at first for sobs. Finally she managed to get out: 'He said… he said… I was a sodding spastic. I shouldn't be at their school. I should be at a special school with other spastics. He said… he said… they didn't want me in their class.'

I comforted her as best I could, while grief and fury writhed inside me. I was also profoundly shocked. Previously the children had been young and probably unthinkingly cruel, but now they were older, in their early teens, and it had to be intentional. It seemed so especially vicious to ring her in her home, her private fortress. I am sure it must be the same these days for those who are bullied on their mobiles or over the internet. It is far, far worse than being bullied at school because it penetrates into your whole life and your private self. There is no escape.

Yet even this we did not report to the school.

Spratty had another rather traumatic experience about this time. It was the day for the class to have a check-up at the dentist's, after which they could go home. They were allowed to go as a group without an escort, and they were examined by the dentist in alphabetical order. Spratty was next to last but, ever anxious to please and also being kind by nature, she allowed the last-girl-but-one to go before her because she was in a hurry. Spratty was therefore last to leave. She saw the others were waiting for a bus at the bus-stop, but she hung behind so that she would take the next bus. This was not because she did not wish to join them but because by now she was acutely aware that the others were embarrassed to be seen with her in public.

When she got on the bus to take her to the bus station where she would change buses for home, she realized to her dismay that she had no ticket and no money to buy one with.

'I'm sorry,' she said to the bus driver. 'I've just found I don't have any money. What shall I do?'

The bus driver studied her.

'OK,' he said. 'It doesn't matter. Go and sit at the back.'

Spratty thanked him and sat down at the back in great relief. Since she still did not have any money for the next bus and that driver might not be as understanding, she sensibly decided to walk the short way to the university from the bus station, find Mike whom she knew was teaching there that day, and get some money from him.

The bus reached the end stop at the bus station in Helsinki. Everyone got off. Spratty at the back was of course last and before she could get off, the bus driver shut the door.

'Can you open it again, please?' said Spratty, thinking he hadn't noticed her.

'Oh, I'm not letting *you* off!' he said.

Spratty was completely taken aback.

'Why not?' she asked.

She had to struggle to get the words out, because when she was upset, as she naturally was now, her muscles tightened up and her speech became less intelligible.

The bus driver didn't answer.

'Where've you come from?' he asked.

'School,' she said. 'I mean, the dentist's. Our class was at the dentist's.'

'What's the name of your school?' he asked.

'The Steiner school.'

'What?'

She repeated it.

'And the name of your teacher?'

She gave it.

'I'm going to ring them,' he said.

He phoned through to his centre and got the number. Spratty, by now in some distress, could hear him asking about her and whether this story was true. The teacher obviously confirmed it, but the bus driver asked to speak to the school nurse. When the school nurse came on the line, he asked her too. Spratty had no idea what she had said, but the driver was still sceptical and kept on looking at her.

'I'm not letting you go home alone,' he said.

Spratty tried to explain.

'I'm going to see my father. At the university. He'll give me the money to buy my ticket to get home.'

'I'm not letting you go alone,' the driver repeated. 'I don't know that you can cope. I'm going to ask the town authorities to come and get you and take you home.'

So Spratty waited helplessly in the bus. With each moment that passed, her sense of humiliation became greater. She did not know why the driver was doing this, and possibly did not want to face thinking of the probable reason, as it would humiliate her further.

When the social security people (or whoever they were) rolled up in their car, Spratty was already so mortified that she would not tell them where she lived because she was not – she was *not* – going to be driven home in what she saw as public disgrace. She finally convinced them to drop her off at the university where her father worked, which they presumably checked.

When she got there, she half-ran to the teachers' room, then looked in the teachers' café. There she saw Mike sitting over a cup of coffee, the inevitable cigarette in his hand, correcting papers. Her sense of being saved was profound. Mike was as usual unfazed and comforting. He sat her down over an orangeade and a bun, calmed her down, gave her some money for the fare home, and then went off to lecture on the poet Milton.

When I saw Spratty later, she gave me a cut-down version of the incident and did not say how much it had upset her. We agreed that the man had probably only meant to be kind. Behind these words we both knew the probable realities: yes, he had no doubt meant it for the good, but behind it was the usual reaction of slurred speech meaning a slurred mind; he may have thought that this girl who had no money had possibly run away from an institution and it was his duty to see that she was cared for and not allowed to wander around on her own. He probably told the story back home as an example of a good deed – and so it was in intention. The effect on Spratty, however, was that she felt deep humiliation and always made sure thereafter that she carried either a bus ticket or the exact fare.

The bullying at school, however, was soon to stop. But ironically for a reason to which bullying would have been preferable.

CHAPTER 12

We had recently agreed we had to move. Spratty and Johnny shared a room, but now they were fourteen and twelve we decided that they had to have rooms of their own. Furthermore, although my mother had died three years earlier and no longer came to stay with us, Mike's bachelor brother Philip now came for several weeks each year. We had only rented our flat and felt it was time we bought something of our own. I had recently been left a small unexpected legacy by an uncle, and with that as a downpayment we would be able to get a mortgage. After months of house-hunting, we had found a typically Finnish small wooden house that we could just about afford. It was outside Helsinki in what was then more or less the countryside. Although a lot needed to be done – it had no hot water, the cold water was pumped from a well, and there was only a wood-burning stove in the kitchen – we fell in love with it. It also had a big, wildish garden and a direct bus a short walk away which went past the children's school. It was also very close to a railway line which would take Mike and me into Helsinki and to work. We took out a large mortgage, bought it and then started to install a proper kitchen and hot water, though mains water would have to wait until we could afford it. Meanwhile, Mike, who loved doing things with his hands, gradually began to put up shelves and bookcases and take bits of our furniture out there when he had time. We had planned to move in the Christmas vacation, so as to give us time to pack up the flat and settle in to the new house before the new term started in mid-January. Gradually the rows of banana and apple boxes grew into stacks along the walls of our flat. Along with them were stronger boxes rented from the removals firm, who were coming to collect them and everything else on a Monday in mid-December.

On the Saturday, Mike was carrying a load down to the car when he had a cerebral bleed. He was rushed to hospital, but died in the early hours of Monday morning, and when the removals men knocked on the door at 8 a.m., I had to tell them that my husband had died three hours ago and we would have to cancel or postpone the removals. Earlier that morning I had had to tell the children. It was, quite without exception, the worst thing I have ever had to do in my life.

It was just before Christmas, and Mike's funeral was held two days before Christmas Eve. Throughout we were of course surrounded by boxes and had to open them to find the glasses, cups, knives and forks, etc. and anything at all we needed to use. It was a strange nightmare through which I passed in a semi-conscious state while our many friends and colleagues rallied round and simply took over our lives for the moment. My sole anxiety was to help the children get through it.

Of course the reason for our move had now gone: there was an all-too-free room. The flat owner kindly told us we could stay on if we wanted, and as for the house, it could be resold. I consulted Spratty and Johnny and we unanimously decided to move. Our reasons were partly because we all felt that Mike had been getting the house ready for us – I still have his plans for what should go where – and partly because we felt that in the flat we would always miss his presence, we would look into his room and he would not be there correcting papers. In the new house we would feel he was there because he had been preparing it for us. He would want us to be there.

I can remember little about the two weeks or so before we left the flat. I know I drank innumerable cups of tea with lots of sugar. I didn't like sugar in tea, but my mind fixed on the memory that sweet tea was good for shock, and I was aware without directly knowing it that I was in shock. I didn't cry to start with, and not for several days afterwards, until one afternoon I had gone to a local supermarket to do the shopping – for our lives had to continue as normally as I could manage – when, standing in a queue for the check-out, I felt the tears begin to pour down my face uncontrollably. I paid blindly and carried my bags down to my car parked in the underground car-park. There, sitting at the steering-wheel in my motionless car, the tears became tearing sobs and I rested my chest on the wheel as they went on and on, seemingly forever. I don't know how long I spent in the gloom of that car-park, buried in it. By the time I got back home, I had controlled myself again and was dry-eyed.

Meanwhile, Mike's brother Philip had arrived the day after his death. He had been due to come for Christmas anyway but now, instead of a happy time with his family, he faced the bitter grief of the loss of his beloved brother, perhaps his only really close friend ever since childhood. He too must have been in the same shocked, trance-like state, and he was staying in a room surrounded by reminders of Mike: his desk, papers, ashtrays – all of which had been left for last-minute packing. He was an even more reticent man than Mike and he spoke nothing about his pain. I don't even know if he ever asked himself the age-old question: 'Why? Why Mike?' Many people have questioned me since about whether I have asked that too, and have seemed amazed and unbelieving when I say 'No', as if they've thought it was something I must have felt but have forgotten or buried deep inside me. But I never did, any more than I asked myself that question when Spratty was born with cerebral palsy, because in both cases the answer must be the same: 'Why not?' – and that is a question that can have no answer.

The funeral also passed by me with only flashes of later memory: the children, Philip and I sitting in the front row of the church while person after unrecalled person came up to put flowers on the coffin, bowing towards us as they made way for others, as is the custom at funerals in Finland; a snaking line of silent people edging the long path up from the church, through the gate into the churchyard, and turning towards the open grave under the tree, waiting; the face of an English girl who had been looking after the children earlier the only one actually in focus in the crowd and later remembered; the gathering in the university teachers' room afterwards with that mixture of social party and sadness that characterizes funeral baked meats; a small choir of colleagues singing, people recalling Mike's wit, and much laughter at the memories.

Christmas Day is also a blur with flashed recollections: a friend's house and as normal a Christmas as we could manage; the shudder of grief shrugged off as the children unwrapped presents that were supposed to come from us both; the new dressing-gown for Mike that I had already bought for him, now given to Philip, and Philip's face as he looked down at it; a silly joke I made in the car when an unusually glowing sunset lit up the sky about Mike's permanent cigarette having set fire to his white robes in heaven and all of us giggling: tears and laughter can have the same trigger.

And all the time in the background of everything were boxes, boxes, boxes, as Philip left sadly to go back to work in England and we waited to move.

So just before a snowy New Year, on a day when packed ice made the dirt road on the slight hill up to the house almost impassable, our university colleagues banded together and moved us. They too were grieving for Mike, who was much respected and liked by all.

That New Year's Eve was a bright moonlit night. We had bought some rockets, and, determined to go on as before and to celebrate what we hoped would prove an infinitely happier new year, we let off some fireworks in the deep snow of the garden. Then at midnight the three of us went out onto the tiny wooden balcony on the top floor. Our house was at that time surrounded by thick forests of pine, birch and spruce. We had heard or seen no other rockets but ours and could see no lights. It was as if we were marooned in a sea of snow and dark branches.

We counted 'One, two, three!' together and then called out in Finnish and Swedish: 'Happy New Year!'

It was our statement of hope to the world.

Suddenly, out of the darkness, faint voices called back to us in both languages: 'Happy New Year!'

We went back inside, feeling a little less alone.

CHAPTER 13

They say that the three most stressful things in life are death, divorce and moving. We experienced two at once. Maybe, though, the fact that we were forced to be so extremely busy and create a new home and life from the banana and apple boxes that had filled our floors was some kind of therapy for our grief. We were forced to regain some kind of normality: Spratty and Johnny had to go back to school, using their new bus route; while I had to return to work at the university and also to continue to meet the deadlines for the textbooks teaching English as a second language which had unexpectedly become my second and parallel career. This was now also a desperately necessary one, as from then on I had to pay off alone the large mortgage we had taken out, not to speak of the ordinary expenses which Mike and I had previously shared. It would have been quite impossible on just my university salary. I was lucky indeed to have so much work, I realized, because when working I was forced to concentrate and not think of grief or loss.

We had been a close and loving family. Mike had been devoted to his children and they to him. In those days the idea of counselling for those who had experienced a death in the family – or anything else for that matter – had not been introduced. We each coped in our own particular ways. Johnny was very quiet, spending long hours in his room reading or listening to music; Spratty on the other hand went into a whirl of rushing round to visit people, phoning them, immersing herself in activities of any kind. She had a desperate need to talk to others. She became very active in the Scouts and made several friends there, among whom was one, Sussi, who was going to be a huge support to her in the future. It only struck me later how strange it was that it had been impossible for her to make close friends at school and yet how easy it seemed once she was outside it. It was as if school was a totally different and alien world. She also joined a youth group from a local Finnish Lutheran church, and went on a first aid course. The youth group was particularly important, as they were all of her own age and offered her their friendship and psychological support without reserve. This took care of a lot of her evenings, and on those evenings that she was home, she read through an entire pile of books she had borrowed off a girl at school before finally going to sleep.

I concentrated on work, but tried to arrange it so that I did it away from home or when Johnny and Spratty were at school: I had always held to the idea that, if I was home, then I must be available to the children. I did a lot of cooking too, as I had always found it relaxing.

There had been another reason for Spratty's reactions and for her being out of the house that I learned much later. At some point after Mike's death, I had begun to work on a textbook with a colleague of his, an artist and illustrator, whom I had hardly known beforehand. From talking about work, we began to talk about ourselves and many other things: politics, art, beliefs, relationships and so on. Adam was a gifted and interesting man who had the rare ability to be an attentive and sympathetic listener, as well as enjoying long and often provocative discussions face to face or on the phone. He eventually became a close friend and we would ring each other most days to share our thoughts and the day's experiences. The calls would usually be at night, as I did not want them to interfere with my time with the children.

I gradually became dependent on these calls as a kind of lifeline. My friendship with Adam did not affect my love for Mike or my relationship with him, but it had everything to do with my grief and what I had lost. I was able once again to share my thoughts on an almost daily basis, to have fascinating discussions on a vast range of topics with a well-read adult, to seek advice, to experience a male mind's workings again, to feel my own mind stimulated, and almost to forget for the moment my permanent but unspoken grief. We met frequently for work and sometimes for lunches or just a cup of tea or coffee, although he very seldom came to visit us.

It was not until much, much later that Spratty told me that she had been quite sure I was going to marry Adam and could not bear the thought. From her bedroom she could hear my voice talking, although not what I said, and often would not go to sleep until she heard the click of the telephone receiver being put down. So she spun off on her round of visits and activities in her free time from school in order to take her mind off the whole idea.

I don't know at what point Spratty realized that Adam was not a threat and that he was not moving into our lives in the way she had feared. The relationship between us both gradually changed, as relationships do, though he remained and remains a close friend, as does his family. Time took over and my dependence lessened; the phone calls became less frequent, though still as long and detailed whenever they were made. My work called me away more from Finland – brief visits because of the children, but an opening up of my world. I no longer needed a lifeline in the same way.

I would never talk about 'getting over' the death of someone much loved. You don't. Neither my children nor I will ever 'get over' Mike, because it is never over. It is always somewhere deep in the background; but you do get used to the fact, learn to accept it, adjust your life to it; you eventually smile at the memories, remember the joys, and learn to live once again. In this sense, you might say I woke up, I became alive.

Spratty also learned to adjust to life without a father, hard though it was. She still regrets not having known him fully, adult to adult, being able to go to him for advice on her problems, sympathy and comfort in her sorrows, or for him to rejoice with her in her joys. He remains the missing piece in all our jigsaw lives.

One thing we all did immediately after Mike's death, though, and still do, was to talk about him a great deal. He was a very witty man and we would remember his sayings and jokes and laugh a lot over them too. You might say that in this way we kept him alive and present with us. Then, too, my children began to become my confidantes as they grew older, one of the unexpected lights in the blackness of Mike's death being that it drew us closer together. I discussed problems and situations with them in a way that I would not have done had he been alive, as I would no doubt have discussed them with him instead. So they became less my children and more my equals. We were no longer adults and children, but all adults together.

Another strange upside to his death was that the bullying of Spratty stopped from that moment onwards. She was ignored – but she wasn't teased or bullied. Did it stop because now, with her father's death, she was marked out in a way her schoolmates could understand, identify themselves with and sympathize with her at last? Did her teachers speak to the class and tell them that they must all be kind to her? Did their parents? Or was it a combination of all of these? At least from now on she was no longer called a 'sodding spastic'.

CHAPTER 14

The sudden absence of bullying at school did not mean that Spratty's problems were all over. Up to now, her method of defence, her whole attitude to life, had been that there was nothing she could not do because there was nothing at all wrong with her.

One afternoon, she was standing in the kitchen looking out into the garden. She turned as I came in and I saw that her usually smiling face was serious, her eyes large and sad.

'I've a handicap, haven't I,' she said.

I went over to her, put my arms around her, while my throat tightened

'Yes, darling,' I said. 'Not a big one, though. Not a big one.'

We stood there together. I was infinitely sad, yet I knew that this was a moment that had to come – that it was necessary that it came. At some point she needed to acknowledge her handicap and to accept it, so that in the end she could put it aside.

We sat down and I went over her story with her, this time as an adult.

'How does it show?' she asked.

'Well,' I said, 'when you walk, you kick one foot at a bit of an angle. And when you get tense or worried about something, one side of your mouth sort of tightens, and then when you're tired your speech can get a bit slow and you slur your words slightly.'

'Yes,' she said.

'But it's not very much really,' I said. Then, to lighten things a bit, I added: 'Anyway, maybe it's just as well you speak slowly because otherwise there'd be no stopping you!'

'True enough!' she said.

We both laughed because we were both great talkers.

'What about some speech therapy?' I asked. 'Shall we try again?'

We had earlier tried to find her a private speech therapist, since the state had been unable to provide her with one because of the shortage. We had thought it would be important that she could have the therapy in English, and we had been lucky enough to find the daughter of an English friend who was bilingual and a trained speech therapist. However, we had reckoned without Spratty's resistance to the idea that she had any kind of problem at all. This weighted the odds heavily against the therapist being able to help very much, and eventually we had all decided that there was little point in going on with it.

It had been the same with the suggestion of any form of physiotherapy. Here there had been another emotion in play, though, which Mike and I had not realized. As she told me much later: 'One of the things the teasing and bullying at school had done was to make me believe that outsiders couldn't bear to touch me really.'

I still feel pain at this thought.

However, the incident on the bus, which had happened when she was younger, had had one good effect: it had made up her mind to have speech therapy. We decided to make another attempt and this time found a therapist, Diana Diesen, who lived reasonably near us.

One of the most valuable things Spratty learned from her was that she had been breathing in the wrong way: she had been distending her diaphragm when breathing out and tightening it when breathing in, so that her breathing was very shallow. This probably also made her asthma worse – another problem she had had since the age of four. Gradually Diana taught Spratty to reverse her breathing pattern and to have more control over her breath, so that her speech became clearer. This was most noticeable on the telephone, but friends who had not met her for a few months also began to comment on the improvement.

The speech therapist did more for her than this. As Spratty said later: 'She was outside our circle. An adult. My own. I talked to her a lot and particularly I talked to her a lot about Daddy and his death. But about other things too.'

I understood very well, as in their own way my endless phone calls after Mike's death had performed the same function for me.

Despite the improvement in her breathing and speech, she did still have a noticeable speech defect, particularly when she was nervous or tense. This could cause problems, on the telephone and elsewhere. One day a bit later, for instance, she was in the centre of Helsinki and decided to have a hamburger. When she entered the hamburger place, however, a doorman came up to her.

'You can't come in here,' he said.

'Why ever not?' she asked, astonished.

'Because you're drunk,' he said. 'You can't come in here.'

'But I'm not drunk,' she protested. 'I haven't had anything at all to drink.'

'Oh yes you have,' he said. 'Don't give me that! You're drunk. Come on, out!'

Furious but helpless, she left. She tried another place, but exactly the same thing happened. Of course, in Finland doormen are on the look-out for drunks and always suspicious, but a young girl on her own at lunch-time is surely a less likely suspect than many.

When Spratty came home she told me what had happened. She was still incensed, but this time she was determined not to let things lie. Maybe for the first time she realized that there was a fight to be put up on behalf of the handicapped to open people's eyes to their frequent mistreatment.

'I shall write to the papers,' she said.

She did. She mentioned the name of the hamburger chain, what had happened, her age, how humiliating it had been, and said that she felt doormen should be trained to tell the difference between those who are drunk and those who have a speech defect. She got a public apology – and free hamburger vouchers.

Something else occurred, though, which made us realize that a speech defect is not always a disadvantage.

It was her sixteenth birthday. I was waiting for her to come home from school, so that the three of us could have a birthday celebration. When she didn't come back at the time I expected, I was not at first anxious. As the time dragged on, I began to become a little worried. Mobile phones were not in existence at that time, but ever since Mike's death we were all careful to tell one of the others where we were and when to expect us home. Parents frequently ask their children to do this, but now my children asked me, too. From the moment Mike died we knew forever that the unexpected can happen, that plans can be overturned in a second, never to say *when* we would do something but always *if*. To begin with we were anxious if the expected person was even five minutes late, though gradually we learned to quell our anxiety and be more rational. If we were much delayed, though, we always rang. Now, however, when Spratty was over an hour late returning from school, I began to fret. A bus accident? My imagination began to run over various scenarios: being rung by the school, the hospital, the police. I tried to concentrate on preparing our birthday supper and then suddenly, to my huge relief, I heard the front door bang.

'That you, sweetie?' I called out. 'What made you so late?'

She ran into my arms and I knew that something was very wrong. She didn't cry – she was probably too shocked to cry – and it was a time before she got her story out.

'I was coming back home,' she said. 'You know – along the road from the bus-stop.'

The bus she took to and from school ran along the main road from which there was about a ten-minute walk along a minor road until she would turn into our little lane, flanked by birch trees.

'I was walking along there,' she said, 'and a car stopped by me. There was a man in it and he asked if he could give me a lift. I said "No", that my home was just a few minutes away.' She paused. 'But he opened the door and told me to get in.'

I waited. Like any other parents, we had of course warned our children about taking lifts or accepting sweeties from strangers, but mainly we had warned them about the dangers in England. Such things didn't happen in Finland. Yet she did know of the dangers and I thought: 'Well, it's all right because she's here now.'

'And I got in,' she said.

'What!' I said. 'But…'

She started to shake and to cry. 'I knew I shouldn't do it. I knew. But – but – I can't explain. There was nobody else around, no cars, no walkers and even if I had tried to scream, I couldn't. I couldn't get a sound out. I couldn't move. It was as if I was paralysed, hypnotized, like a rabbit with a snake. So when he told me again to get in, I did.'

'And did he drive you here then?' I asked, hoping – for how had she got here?

'No,' she said. 'I told him where to go, but he went the other way. And we just drove on. I told him again where I lived and asked him to go back, but he didn't. And I didn't know what to do.'

I waited in terror for her to go on.

'And then – we'd got quite far – he suddenly stopped the car and told me to get out. So I did. I knew sort of where I was but there weren't any buses or anything, so I just ran and walked as fast as I could all the way home.'

'And – that was it?' I asked.

'Yes, he drove off.'

'Thank God for that,' I said.

'You know what, Mummy,' she said.' I think the reason he stopped and let me out was that he didn't like my speech defect.'

I never thought I would ever be grateful – and so overwhelmingly grateful – that she had one.

It was pointless to read her a lecture about the dangers of taking lifts with strange men – her experience had certainly been enough to show her that. But after we had had a cup of tea and calmed ourselves, I said I must ring the police.

'What kind of car was it?' I asked. 'What did it look like?'

'I didn't really notice. I wasn't thinking,' said Spratty. 'Dark red maybe. Not very big. I should have noticed more. Sorry.'

'It's OK, darling. Did you notice what the man was like?'

'Not young. Middle-aged. But, you see, I was so frightened I couldn't take him in. I didn't want to look at him.'

Yes, I understood. That was how it must be for those children and young people who did get into cars with strangers, even though they knew they mustn't. It must be as Spratty had said: they were too hypnotized by fear to do anything or notice much. She had been one of the lucky ones.

I phoned the police and described what had happened.

'How old is your daughter?' the policeman at the other end of the telephone asked.

'Sixteen today,' I said.

'Ah,' said the policeman. 'He's up to his old tricks, is he? There was a man around here three years ago, picking up girls of your daughter's age. We thought he'd stopped.'

I was taken aback by this casual attitude to the affair.

'Right,' said the policeman. 'We'll keep an eye out for him.'

And that was the end of that. I suppose I had thought they would instantly send out a patrol car, or at least come and ask Spratty some questions, but we never heard anything more. However, it was not a comfortable feeling to know that a man 'up to his old tricks' was around, and for some time afterwards I went to the bus-stop to pick Spratty up if she was going to come home alone.

CHAPTER 15

There were not many of these trips to school left, because we were about to move to England for a while, perhaps for good. Mike had always intended us to return to England when he retired, which would have been eight years before I did. Spratty and Johnny were still British, and they had been born and brought up in Finland simply because we happened to live and work there. Now that they were aged sixteen and fourteen I thought they should have the chance to decide for themselves where they wished to continue their education and to spend their adult lives. So we let our house to a Finnish family for nine months and packed up once again.

I had arranged to go to St Albans, just north of London. Here we had great friends whose children were almost exactly the same age as mine and through whom we could get advice about schools and renting a house. Spratty went to the local girls' comprehensive and Johnny to a local school for boys. It took them both about a week to adjust but after that they both enjoyed the experience, so very different in many ways from their school back in Finland.

Johnny was very struck by the fact that he had to call his teacher 'Sir' and by the strict discipline. To begin with he also suffered from a language problem. Not that his English was not as good as that of any British youngster of his own age – but he spoke it with a different accent. Both Spratty and Johnny had acquired their English from Mike and me and our friends, many of whom were teachers of English. We spoke it in what was called then 'Received Pronunciation' but which was also perceived as 'posh' or (then) as 'BBC English'. We were also an older generation as well: time had moved on and English pronunciation with it. Even 'posh' English was now pronounced in a slightly different way by the young, and indeed most British people spoke English with very different types of pronunciation. They always had done so in fact, but the difference was that now regional accents were accepted or even preferred. Consequently Johnny's perceived 'posh' English was the subject of teasing and laughter when he arrived. Johnny typically refused to change it, joked, and after a week his mates accepted him as he was. They even defended him. One day he was in a cricket match against another school (he had, perhaps surprisingly, learned to play cricket in Helsinki in the Helsinki Cricket Club). Before they started, one of his classmates warned him: 'And for God's sake, don't open your mouth – they'll kill you!'

For Spratty, her speech was marked by her defect, so her type of pronunciation was not really noticed. Her only problem was that her school had decided to put her into a lower form than her age group. This was not because of her handicap but because under the English school system her peers were ahead of her in some things and were also due to take their O-level exams. She found herself in many ways more mature than her classmates and certainly with a wider general knowledge and knowledge of world affairs than the rest. Like Johnny, she was also amazed that she had to call her teachers Mrs or Mr Somebody, and not by their first names, as she had done in Finland. She also found school much more formal and the discipline stricter. Nonetheless she was not bullied or teased at all; she was happy and made one or two good friends with whom she remained in touch for several years.

The one irksome thing for them both was my insistence that they could not walk or cycle home alone at night, but must always be fetched or take a taxi. To begin with, they could not understand this, as they had been used to returning home at night quite freely in Finland.

'But why?' they asked.

'It's just not safe here in England. The population is so huge and there are nutters amongt them. You never know.'

'Oh, Ma! You're just over-protective. We're not children any more.'

'It's not that,' I said. 'Teenagers are at risk too. Do you think I like saying it? I'm so sad that this has happened to England. But you just ask your mates at school. Other parents have warned me.'

And they did indeed learn that others of their own age in St Albans had the same rules, so they reluctantly agreed to go by them too.

I was meanwhile working full-time on a textbook series for the British publisher Longman. Their headquarters were in Harlow, about an hour's drive from St Albans, and this had been another reason for my choice of living there. When the children were at school, my days were spent writing or in visiting the publisher, so I had little time during the day for socializing; in the evening and at the weekend I wanted to be with Spratty and Johnny as much as I could. They had homework of course – a lot more than they had got in Finland – which they did when they got home; then after a meal together we usually wanted to sit down and watch TV. To begin with, though, there was a snag: the house we had rented was a modern terraced house and fully furnished, but 'fully furnished' turned out not to include a TV. I decided to rent one, as it was not worth buying a new one for only a few months.

It was now that I got my first shock about how things were done in England.

'Do you rent out TV sets?' I asked a man in a local TV shop.

'Yes, madam, we do.'

'We've just moved into the area from abroad for part of this year, you see,' I said.

'Of course, madam. How long would you be wanting it for?'

I told him and he calculated the rental rate for a small TV set. It was all fixed – until we came to the contract.

'I'll want your husband's signature of approval on this contract, of course.'

'What!' I said.

'I'm afraid we don't rent out TVs unless we have the husband's signature.'

'But I'm a widow!' I protested. 'How can I have my husband's signature?'

He seemed a bit nonplussed, but said: 'I'm sorry, madam, I can't let you have the TV without it. Those are our rules.'

I was incredulous. Just how far had equality for women reached in England, if at all? I thought of those single mothers, widows, elderly women – all unable to afford to buy a TV and therefore deprived of one simply because a lone man could rent a TV but they could not. I was not going to be one of them! Somebody needed to put up a fight about this.

I drew myself up to my full height and put on my most authoritative tone. I felt rather like Bertie Wooster's Aunt Agatha in P.G. Woodhouse books.

'Now, look,' I said. 'I am a widow, yes. But I'm a widow in full-time permanent employment. I'm a lecturer at a university. I have a salary. I have a bank account here. There is no reason on this earth why you should not rent out a TV to me.'

He began to get a bit rattled. 'But the rules...'

'Bugger the rules,' is what I wanted to say but didn't. Aunt Agatha would not have done so. Instead, I said, 'Can I speak to the manager, please?'

Reluctantly, he called to a man out back. I explained the situation and then I said: 'Now what I want you to do is to pick up that phone and ring my bank manager here in St Albans. He will assure you that my bank balance is good for the rental of a TV for eight months.'

The two men were rather shame-faced by now, but they did what I said. The upshot was that I walked away with a contract for the rental of a TV, not approved by a husband. I felt I had struck a blow for Women's Lib – but I continued to be appalled that such a situation could arise at all.

There were few signs of Women's Lib in St Albans. All the women with young children I met seemed to have given up their jobs with their first baby; anyway, there was little or no provision for child care even if they wanted to go on working. Women of my age did sometimes have part-time jobs, but by then they had missed the boat as far as a career went. What struck me most was that a great many seemed to accept their destiny as permanent housewives as if it were pre-ordained, as did the men. No doubt some women were perfectly happy in this role, but for the others there was no real choice. Spratty was also surprised that most of the girls in her class did not seem to consider having a career except to fill the gap between school and marriage. It was only to her friends that she let on that she wanted to be a doctor.

One of the other things that struck us all was the amount of coverage given by the TV and newspapers to murder, violence and sex scandals, often putting them first on the TV news. In Finland they were not usually given as much publicity, at least in the main daily papers, and were most often the subject of short notices on the inside pages. As for the sexual irregularities of politicians or other prominent people, they were usually considered fairly unimportant, just as they were in France. In England, it seemed, governments could fall because of a minister's affair with his secretary.

Spratty was certainly struck, too, by her schoolmates' attitude to nudity and sex in general. Any reference to them or to a related word such as 'breast' seemed to arouse a kind of prurient snigger. She was astonished to find the girls in her class refused to undress in front of each other. Early on, she remarked: 'You know the girls at school are really weird – they're too embarrassed to take their clothes off in front of each other. Isn't that weird? I mean, it isn't as if there were any boys around.'

'Is it still like that? Good heavens!' I said. 'It was like that in my day. I even had a friend who went to a school where they had to take a bath dressed in a nightie. I thought things must have changed by now.'

'No,' she said. 'I told them about Finnish saunas and how women of all ages had a sauna together with nothing on – even if they didn't know each other, either. They thought it was revolting!'

'But what do they do then these days about showers after gym or sports? Do they have separate cubicles?'

'Oh, they don't shower,' Spratty said. 'On gym days they just go to school with their gym clothes under their uniforms and then take the uniform off to do gym. Then they put the uniform on again afterwards.'

'You mean that they go on wearing their sweaty gym clothes under their uniforms for the rest of the day?' I asked, completely forgetting I had done the same at school. 'Now I would call *that* revolting!'

'So do I,' she said. 'Disgusting. I'd like to see how they'd react in a sauna, though. But anyway, they seem to think that saunas are somehow – well – something naughty, sexy. I told them real saunas weren't, but they wouldn't believe me.'

'Mm,' I said. 'I think they do have a bad reputation here – you see saunas advertised in phone booths here along with so-called "massage parlours" and prostitutes' addresses.'

'Weird,' she said.

Yet although many things were 'weird', they both discovered that part of them slotted very happily and naturally into English life. It was as if their genes were at home. As the days grew longer and the summer term drew to an end, the time was also coming round for the decision about where we would live from now on. We hadn't talked about it before, and I wondered a little what their decision about countries was going to be.

'Well, which is to be for us – Finland or England?' I finally asked.

They hesitated. I knew they were wondering which I wanted.

'What do you think, Mum?' asked Spratty. 'Which do you want?'

'No,' I said. 'I want this to be your decision and not mine. And if you are thinking about me – well, I truly don't mind. There are advantages and disadvantages for me about both. I don't have to go on working at Helsinki University, you know.'

They looked at each other.

'We've been talking about it, and, if you really don't mind...'

'Come on, out with it!' I said.

'Finland!' they both said in unison.

'OK,' I said. 'Finland it is. Why did you decide that?'

'Well, all my mates are there in my class,' said Johnny.

'And all our really close friends are there,' added Spratty.

'And the house.'

'Yes, our yellow house. The one that Daddy got ready for us.'

Their decision came in the end as a relief to me. I had been lonely in St Albans despite my friends. People were not unkind – indeed they were often very welcoming – but it was there I became profoundly conscious of my single state for the first time, as if half of me was missing.

'Even the ducks here go around in pairs,' I had complained bitterly.

So we returned to Finland, to our home and to their school, where Spratty still had about two years to go before she would take the Finnish matriculation examination and leave school. To do what?

CHAPTER 16

As far as Spratty was concerned, the 'what' was going to be the same as she had decided at eleven: she would be a doctor. It still seemed to most people an impossibility, even if her speech and co-ordination had improved considerably. But then some people had also been sure she would not be able to drive. She had of course been very anxious to drive the moment she reached eighteen, as it would be yet another proof of her capacity to be and do exactly the same as others. When she told her classmates she was going to take driving lessons, one of them said: 'You? They'll never let you drive!'

I too had wondered a little if she would have the co-ordination needed for driving, but of course sent her off to a driving school nonetheless. The driving instructor was brilliant.

'Well,' he said, 'let's go off to the stadium car-park first and we'll see if you would need an automatic.'

'An automatic car' was all he said – not a word about the possibility of not being able to drive at all. They went off. After a while, the instructor had said: 'You'll be fine.

You don't need an automatic at all – you'll be fine with ordinary gears.'

When Spratty told me, I could have hugged that man. It was such a boost to her confidence that an expert could tell she could do it like everybody else. Soon she was happily driving my car and doing it well, with that sense of freedom and independence that driving can give. For her, though, came the additional knowledge that she was demonstrating both her physical and mental equality with anyone else.

Being a doctor was of course a different goal, but her close family, long experienced by now in her will, determination and capacity to do the impossible, no longer ruled it out completely. What concerned me more was her command of the subjects needed to get into medical school in the first place, especially chemistry. We knew good grades in chemistry were a must for medicine, but she had not managed to achieve these at school. Many people will say they were 'bad at' a subject at school, but the reasons can be very varied: perhaps a child does not like the teacher, perhaps it is 'fashionable' in the class not to like or work at the subject, the child may miss an important week and never catch up with some basic piece of knowledge, the teacher may be poor at teaching in some way or at inspiring enthusiasm for the subject, the child may simply not do the necessary work required to keep up with the others, or their tastes and inclinations – including those of their friends – may lie elsewhere.

Personally I think it is very seldom that a child without other problems is born not good at a subject from the very start. Nor, it turned out, was Spratty innately bad at chemistry. We were later to discover that what was wrong was that she had not acquired an understanding of what underlies chemistry, so she could only learn by rote. A basic understanding of a subject is what teaching and learning is all about, be it maths, grammar, a language, punctuation or anything else. If you don't understand why, you can't understand how.

We sat down together and discussed the medical school options. Spratty's trilingual background was now an immense advantage, because it enabled her to apply to medical schools in three countries: Finland, Sweden and Britain. In each country medicine was renowned for being the most difficult subject to get in to study – but then Spratty always did choose Everest. Her preference was for Helsinki, near her family and friends, or then another Finnish university; but Britain was also a good option, and Sweden a possibility too. The intake systems were different in each country: Finnish medical school entrance simply involved getting top marks in an examination; in Britain it involved interviews, as well as top results in the A-level examinations. Since under the British system applications were made before taking the final A-level examinations, we decided the sensible thing to do was to apply there first. Here we met another hitch, a financial one. Although Spratty was a British citizen, she lived abroad and therefore would be counted as a foreign student by most of the British universities. This would mean paying full fees, which I was unable to afford. We eventually discovered that Oxford and Dundee Universities would count her as a home student (why some did and some didn't was a mystery we did not try to fathom), so she applied there. Oxford, no doubt intrigued by the peculiarity of her background, called her for an interview, so Spratty flew over to England and turned up for her interview in great excitement.

I blamed myself afterwards for not having prepared her for the type of interview she would get. I had been to Oxford myself and knew that interviews there were not at all like the ones she might expect elsewhere – you were asked unexpected questions, ones that were not necessarily related to your subject at all. Oxford was interested in potential, not what you knew now. It was interested in the ability to think for yourself, to be original, to be open to other ideas and to have interests outside your specialist subject. It was also attracted by the unusual, even the quirky, so the whole interview could be spent discussing things other than the subject you wanted to study. Spratty was totally unprepared for this. Why hadn't we talked about it? Why hadn't I practised such an interview with her? Or was it, as she said later, that I asked her but she wanted to go it alone? As it was, Spratty's interview was short and formal. Undoubtedly then, and quite obviously now, she was a girl with very great potential indeed – but failed to show it. As she said, for one thing she simply did not have the English medical vocabulary needed. Since of course she was also very nervous, her cerebral palsy was more evident than usual. It was no great surprise that Oxford turned her down.

Although I do blame myself for not having prepared her, I strongly believe that life has a definite path for people to take. Even if it does not seem so at the time, the path one thinks one wants may in the end prove not to be the best, and another opens up. It was to be so for Spratty. In the end it was probably much the best thing that she did not get into Oxford after all. Nor did she get into Dundee. Dundee had accepted her on condition that she got three As and two Bs in her matriculation exam, which was equated with English A-levels but was actually based on a different system. We knew in advance that the chances were slim to negligible, as Dundee was measuring by the Scottish A-level exam, which did not quite correspond to the Finnish system either. Although Spratty ended up with a respectable Finnish matriculation certificate, it was without the three As required by Dundee.

This left her with the possibility of Finland or Sweden. Germany, where some Finnish students went, seemed out of the question because it meant yet another language. She tried the Helsinki entrance exam, not with great hope because of her lowish mark in chemistry. She did not get in. She tried Sweden too, but did not get in there either. Friends and family comforted her with the knowledge that most applicants for medical school did not get in on their first try – there was always another year.

There were many people who suggested that instead of medicine she should study something else related to it. Perhaps she might apply to study biology or biochemistry, which were easier to get into, and she might later work in a medical laboratory? Spratty refused all such suggestions. Then what about nursing? Nurses were well trained and highly thought of in Finland, even if – as for nurses everywhere – the pay was low. Spratty would have none of it. She was not interested in the pay, high or low, she wanted to be a doctor and a doctor she would be. She would take the following year's entrance examinations, but meanwhile she would also get some work experience.

CHAPTER 17

Spratty's aim was to get a job connected in some way with medicine or care, so she applied for work in a residential home for the elderly in Helsinki, as an assistant. On the telephone, the employer hesitated. We were used to this, as Spratty's speech defect alone, without the presence of her personality, made people on the other end think she was either drunk or had a mental problem. The employer, however, at least made an appointment for an interview and, once she talked to Spratty in person, had no doubts at all. It was a bit like how she got into play school all over again.

The residents, both singles and couples, had their own rooms or small flats, but ate communally and had communal sitting areas. Spratty would start the coffee, lay the breakfast buffet table, help them with their food, help them to put on their stockings and to dress, find their teeth and hearing aids, see to their medicines and that they took the right dosage, even lead the morning prayers, then reverse the order in the evenings. She would frequently be the sole person on duty at nights. She had by this time taken and passed a first aid course so knew the basic procedures in an emergency. She was – unsurprisingly to her family and friends – very popular with the oldies. She refused to call them by their first names or to use the informal *du* form for 'you' in Swedish, as she knew that their generation was one that had grown up in a more formal society, where first names and *du* were only used among intimates or in an employer–servant relationship. She felt that for her, a young girl, to address them in such a familiar way would take away from their dignity as people. She also treated them with affection, as if she were a surrogate niece, and would often hold their hands or pat them on the shoulder. Not all of them, for not all would like it or wish for it, but for some who had few or no visitors she knew that this was the only affectionate physical contact they had had in years. Her eyes had always been full of feeling, whether merry, sympathetic, hurt or sad; one old man said that was how he would like to die – looking up into her eyes.

Such physical contact would possibly today be considered suspect or even forbidden in some places. People forget how necessary human touch is to the psychological or spiritual well-being of the old as well as the very young. A pat on the hand or a touch on the shoulder is enough to establish a sense of shared humanity, the comfort of feeling that one is not alone. Yet how many of those who live by themselves ever exchange even a handshake with another person?

Unlike many children these days, mine were very used to the elderly. My mother and father had each been one of twelve, so my children had experienced an abundance of great-uncles and great-aunts on our annual journeys to England. Mike had only two aunts and some cousins, but he also valued family ties, and these trips were spent in a round of visits to increasingly ageing relatives. Both our children therefore grew up with a knowledge and understanding of the elderly and a respect and affection for them, despite the comic or sometimes peculiar side of one or two. Most importantly, although the age difference was obviously there and clear, it did not for them turn the middle-aged and old into alien groups with which the young had nothing at all in common. So Spratty was perfectly comfortable with the elderly people in her home.

Coming up again soon, though, were the medical school entrance exams in Finland. She joined a prep course for them and studied as hard as she could. She made a number of friends among the hopefuls sitting the exam for the first, second or even third time – some of them would remain future friends as well. Although it was inevitable that not all would get in, as the intake was very small, they all rooted for each other and after the exam eagerly looked for all their names on the results list. It was an unusually successful group: five out of the seven who applied got in, two did not. Spratty was one of the two. Chemistry had again been her downfall, even if her results were better than last time. She was deeply disappointed but still determined not to give up but to try again next year.

The thought of a re-sit of the exams, though, worried me. I thought her chemistry needed much more work to get her up to the level that was required. I tried to find a 'crammer' in Finland but failed. I knew there were plenty in London, though, and also that there were good and bad ones. I sent off for some brochures and spent hours trying to find clues in them as to what they would be like. Most of them coached school leavers, both from the UK and other countries, and Spratty and I thought that if she stayed a couple of terms she might actually be able to achieve some English A-levels, which would give her a further option of applying again to a British university.

I wished I could visit the crammer's in London and speak to the teachers, but I was working. The fees were fairly outrageous, especially as Spratty would have to be a boarder, but I was getting some extra money now from writing and thought I could afford it for a couple of terms. At least it was worth a try. We picked one almost with a pin and sent her off.

It was nearly a complete disaster. Spratty's room was in a hostel, a house that had been divided up to make as many small rooms for students as possible. Her window was about a foot from a brick wall and most of the window was obscured anyway by a clothes cupboard which would fit nowhere else. The light therefore had to be on all the time. The rest of the room was so tiny that there was no space for anything but a small bed, a desk and a chair. Many a student lives in such accommodation, of course, but the worst thing was that the walls were so thin that even the slightest sound could be heard from the rooms next to hers as well as from those above and below. Her fellow students were not quiet. What they were mostly interested in was parties, so the noise was never-ending: punk from the left, rock from the right, jazz from upstairs and hip-hop from below, and from even further beneath the sound of the underground trains and their doors opening and shutting every time they stopped at Notting Hill tube station.

None of this would have mattered if she had been happy, but she was not.

'Have you made any friends?' I asked her over the phone.

'No,' she said. 'None.'

'Why not?'

'Oh, they're mostly quite a bit younger than me, so we don't talk about the same things in the same way, if you know what I mean. They probably think I'm over the hill. And most of them already have their own friends who they party with.'

Yes, I remembered what a huge difference there is between the young still in their teens and those in their twetnties, when twenty is already over the hill and life a descent into old age after that.

'What about the crammer's?' I asked hopefully. 'What's it like?'

'Pretty hopeless,' she said. 'I don't learn anything really. Most of the other students don't seem at all interested in learning anything and some of the teachers are no good.'

'Well,' I said, speaking as a teacher, 'it must be almost impossible trying to teach a lot of late teenagers who don't want to learn. A nightmare!'

'Oh, I don't think any of the teachers mind much,' she said. 'They get paid and the school makes a lot of money, so who cares?'

'I care!' I said. 'Surely they can see that you at least want to learn something.'

'Oh, they don't think I'm able to learn anything,' she said simply. 'They haven't met anybody like me before. And anyway, the teaching is so different here and the way you have to learn makes it look as if I really am stupid.'

'Why?'

'Well, in biology, for instance, you have to use microscopes and draw leaves. You have to name every single thing on the leaf and be detailed and exact. That's a shock coming from the Steiner school, where exactness was not precisely considered a virtue.'

I laughed, remembering the artistic impressions of leaves that was the Steiner style.

'And then,' she went on, 'you're expected to do essays the English way. I do them in the Finnish way and I'm getting two marks out of twenty for them!'

'How do you mean?' I asked.

'Oh, you know how in Finland you just state facts in essays – what you've read. Here you have to reason, give your own reasons for what you think, your argument and your own conclusions. The comments on my essays are always "Where are your arguments?".'

I thought of the essays written by my Finnish students and my struggle to try to make them not simply regurgitate facts but to think about what they had read and, if necessary, to disagree.

'Isn't there any redeeming feature about it?' I asked desperately.

'Yes,' she said. 'There's one man – the one who teaches chemistry. He interviewed me when I arrived – each subject teacher did – and he was different. He spoke to me in a different way. I enjoy his lessons and I think I'm beginning at last to understand some chemistry.'

'Well, thank God for that!' I said. 'I'm so sorry, darling. I'm sorry I'm so far away and can't help.'

'It's all right, Mummy,' she said, as she always had. 'I'll survive. And there's John. He's wonderful: he takes me out once a week, so then I know at least I'll have a bit of fun and someone to talk to about it and a shoulder to cry on.'

John was her godfather. During our early lives we had been engaged, not once but twice. In the end we had each happily married someone else, but had remained close friends forever after. John and his wife had unfortunately not been able to have any children themselves, so John was Spratty's godfather not only in name but very much in deed. His wife had died a few years before Spratty went to London, and he said he very much enjoyed seeing and talking to her, as up to then he had usually only seen her for a day now and then when we were in Britain. Perhaps because he didn't usually see her on a regular basis he always thought of her as a fragile and delicate being. I could not convince him that although she was sensitive and as easily moved to tears as she was to laughter, she was really pretty tough – she had had to be. He could not imagine why she had set her heart on such a demanding and difficult career as that of a doctor, and at this stage he did not really think she would ever be one anyway. Nonetheless, he was ready to help her in any way he could, and in London he was her lifeline, the only loving, steady and reliable support she had there.

After a term at the crammer's, both Spratty and I decided it was useless and a waste of money to continue. She returned to Finland and home with deep relief. However, the experiment had not been totally in vain because of that one teacher who not only gave her the key to the understanding of chemistry but made her interested in it and even like it; another truth about teaching being of course that if someone becomes interested in a subject, they usually also like it and do well.

CHAPTER 18

When Spratty returned to Finland from London, she still had six months to go before her re-sit of the exams in Helsinki, so she needed a job in between. This time she applied to be an auxiliary nurse at a private hospital in Helsinki. Her duties did not include actual nursing, but it could still be very hands-on indeed, as among other things she had to fetch and empty bedpans for patients, clean up, change the beds, give the patients a blanket bath, or then help them to the lavatory or to have a bath in the bathroom.

Some patients would at first be puzzled and a bit put off by her speech defect. Sometimes they asked her about it. One very cold winter's day, when the temperature outside was −34°C, she was giving an elderly lady a shower.

'Why do you speak like that?' the old lady asked.

Spratty tried to think of a way of explaining simply.

'Well, you see,' she said, 'when I was born I didn't have enough oxygen, so that caused me to have some brain damage. It was in the part which affects speech.'

'Oh dear,' said the lady, looking very concerned. Then she gazed around the bathroom. 'Do you think we should open the window?' she said.

Spratty was almost overcome by giggles, but controlled herself and managed to say: 'No, it's all right. It only mattered then. Not any more.'

She told this story with great glee at home.

I had wondered how Spratty would get on at the hospital, how she would enjoy doing these very menial tasks. I needn't have worried: Spratty was working in a hospital, she was able to watch what doctors were doing, she was perfectly happy.

She also continued to apply to medical schools in Sweden. The Swedish intake system was based on rather different principles. Like Finland, they had no interview system, but it did not solely depend on exam results, because they also considered work experience. It still seems to me ridiculous not to have an interview as part of any medical intake system, unless it is for research alone. The work of doctors puts them in direct contact with people, not only with patients but with their families. Top results in subjects such as maths and other sciences do not mean that you are necessarily good at dealing with human beings, yet most doctoring involves a great understanding of people and their reactions. Doctors need a sensitivity to patients and to their personalities, a quickness of thought as to how to speak to them and phrase what they have to say; they need the ability to break bad news sensitively to them and their relatives, to pick up on facial expression and nuances of speech. 'What kind of person is this?' is surely a question doctors should always ask themselves about a patient. Is the person likely to underestimate or overestimate their symptoms? Do they want the whole truth or an edited version? Should a doctor speak in layman's or medical terms?

It is perhaps the career of all careers that most calls for people who understand and are sensitive to others. It is naturally important that the candidates should be intelligent enough for the long and complicated training they have to undergo and to keep up with their field; but three As at A-level, which usually means automatic acceptance into medical school in Britain, does not make a person more understanding or caring of people. Only a good interviewer can pick out those who are likely to make the best doctors in the end. So why are interviews not part of the selection process everywhere?

However, even if Sweden did not have interviews, to count work experience as part of your merits was at least something. Spratty of course had by now almost three years of experience which counted and also showed her seriousness of purpose: she had worked in a hospital and an old people's home; she had learned first aid; she had been a volunteer with the groups who toured Helsinki on the First of May and Midsummer helping young people who had drunk too much; she had been a keen Scout leader and had looked after young Scouts in camps during the summer; she had shown both leadership and the desire to help and care for others. She had at least a hope of being accepted. She went over to Sweden to make her application. It was her fifth try.

It was now that fate, luck, or Providence stepped in. It came in the shape of Inger. Inger had been one of a sequence of helpers, not exactly au pairs, who had looked after the children in Helsinki when they were young. These people, often students, had mostly been wonderful, and we had been fortunate in being able to offer practice in English as a bonus to the job. Inger was no exception – she was a Swede living in Finland and had wanted a job, at least for a while. During her time with us, Inger became a friend and, though she eventually returned to Sweden, she had remained – and remains – a friend of the family. It was natural, therefore, that Spratty should stay with her in Stockholm, and it was Inger who came with her when she went to the Central University Clearance Administration.

Spratty and Inger sat and waited in the queue. Spratty had once more, as on several previous occasions, been put on the reserve list. She did not entirely understand the Swedish medical intake system, and this time she was determined to find out why she always seemed to be put down as a reserve. Her number was called and she went up to the desk while Inger remained sitting nearby. The official looked through her papers, obviously noting that she had applied before.

He finally looked up. 'No,' he said. 'I'm sorry but these papers won't be enough. You won't be accepted right out with these. Only if a place happens to become free.'

'The wretched chemistry again!' thought Spratty.

She said: 'But I've had a lot of work experience.'

'Yes, I can see,' said the man. 'But I'm afraid it still won't be good enough. We take very few people, you know.'

Spratty knew this all too well. She was about to give up when Inger's voice intervened. She had come over to the desk.

'Does it make a difference that she's English?' she asked.

The man looked surprised, for Spratty had been talking in fluent Swedish.

'Is she?' he said.

'Yes,' said Spratty eagerly. 'I'm British. It's just that I was brought up in Finland and that's why I speak Swedish.'

'Really?' said the man, beginning to look more interested. 'What kind of passport do you have?'

'A British one,' said Spratty. 'I've got it here somewhere.'

She rummaged around and produced it.

'Well, yes,' said the man. 'That does indeed make a difference.'

He studied Spratty's papers again.

'In fact,' he said, 'you have far better papers than we actually require for the Foreigners' Quota. You would have got in long ago had we known.'

To be taken into this small quota, it appeared, you had to have reasonable papers, but you also had to be a citizen of a country outside the Nordic region as well as speaking fluent Swedish – a combination of conditions that was rather rare then. Spratty fulfilled them all. She not only had decent exam results in the necessary subjects in her matriculation but work experience as well.

The next question the man asked was: 'Which university do you want to go to?'

Spratty had considered this earlier but was hardly expecting the question now. She thought quickly. She had really decided that the medical school in the smaller city of Linköping would probably be the best one for her: unusually at the time, its system was one of 'problem-based' learning. This meant that it did not take subjects like anatomy or chemistry as separate courses, but took one organ at a time, like the heart or the lungs, and learned its anatomy and chemistry simultaneously. Spratty thought that might be a more suitable method for an ex-Steiner pupil and that also, as a new system in a smaller university, it might be more accepting of a handicap. However, she had put the Karolinska Institute of Medicine first on her papers at this point and she did not now dare change the order. She knew the Karolinska Institute only as a famous name: it is one of the four major teaching hospitals in Stockholm and its Medical Faculty is also well-known internationally for awarding the Nobel Prize in Medicine. Spratty knew too, her experience at the crammer's in London having forewarned her, that she was likely to be desperately homesick – and Stockholm would be nearer home.

'The Karolinska Institute,' she said.

So the Karolinska Institute it was. Inger left her to continue filling in the necessary papers. Afterwards, Spratty walked back to Inger's flat in disbelieving exhilaration, joy and excitement. From there she rang me where I was staying in London.

'Guess what!' she said.

I knew it was good news, because her voice was always an emotional give-away, but I had no idea about what. I hadn't known she was going to ask about her entrance that day.

'I got in! To the Karolinska Institute,' she said.

'What!'

I could not believe it either. We had waited for it, hoped for it, for so long.

'Really? Really?' I said. 'Oh, how absolutely wonderful!'

We both promptly burst into tears.

When she and I had returned to Finland, we opened a bottle of champagne and drank to a day we had feared might never come.

'Here's to Dr Spratty!' said Johnny.

'And here's to Inger!' said Spratty.

At that moment we all thought that it would be easier-going from now on. We were to find we had been very wrong.

VICTORIA'S STORY

CHAPTER 19

Mum had seen me off on the huge ferry that would take me from Helsinki to Stockholm.

'God bless, Spratty love,' she'd said, sniffing. 'Best of luck – you'll show 'em!'

It was the last time I'd be called Spratty until I was back home. From now on, I was officially Victoria.

The next morning, I woke up to find the ferry winding its way in and out and round the dozens of islands towards Stockholm. I dressed and watched on deck. I wasn't sure how I felt. I'd got into medical school, yes, but I hadn't any idea what lay ahead. I didn't know that much about Sweden, Stockholm, the place where I was going to study, or my fellow students. I didn't even really know where I was going to live.

I'd asked about student accommodation, but I was late off the mark – as usual. Like almost all universities I'd ever heard of, there wasn't enough student accommodation, and most people had to find their own place to live. I'd put myself down on the waiting list for a room in a student hostel. Meanwhile, Mum and I had spread it around that I was looking for somewhere to rent. I'd been told, though, that it was just about impossible for anyone to find a flat to rent. A room in someone's flat or house was the most I could hope for, but again they were very hard to find.

In the end I'd found a room through friends. It was in the house of a Swedish family, but they couldn't have me until the end of the week. So until then I was to stay with another Swedish woman, who was again a friend of friends.

I didn't know much about either of these people except their addresses. From the boat, I found my way with my luggage – lots of it – to the first. Barbro turned out to be a single, middle-aged lady who'd brought up a foster-child earlier but now lived alone.

'Hello!' she said. 'You must be Victoria. I've been told lots about you and I've been so wanting to meet you.'

I liked her at once.

I'd known her American friend and her family rather well in Helsinki, so I felt a little at home – or I would have done if I hadn't known I had to move to other people in four days. I expect Barbro must have been as anxious as me about whether we'd get on, as she didn't usually take in lodgers. We needn't have worried. When the three days were up and she left me at my new address, she whispered: 'Remember, you can always come back if it doesn't work out.'

I felt comforted at once.

Barbro had lived in a modest flat in central Stockholm, not too far away from the institute. The new place was different. I'd imagined from the address that it might be something rather grander, and it was – it was a house in a smart residential area on the outskirts of Stockholm. My hostess welcomed me and took me upstairs.

'This will be your room,' she said. 'I hope it's all right.'

'Yes, lovely,' I said.   ·

I saw they must have made a room especiallyfor me out of a small unused one, as it was mostly filled by a bed and a piano. I wondered where all my bits and pieces would go, but the main thing was that I didn't see a desk, which I knew I'd need. I'd better mention it right now, I thought.

'I'm sorry,' I said. 'But I think I'm going to need somewhere to write – a table or something. I'm so sorry.'

'Oh dear,' she said. 'You can use the kitchen table perhaps. When we're not eating, of course.'

I didn't think the family could have much idea of what studying medicine – or studying at university at all – might mean. The first day, I had gone out to buy some of the books on my book list. The most important one for the term's studies was called *The Cell* – a typical medical reference book, about the size of three red bricks put together and weighing as much. Its price horrified me, and just carrying it back to the house was an effort.

I plonked it on the kitchen table, where my hostess stared at it in amazement.

'You don't have to learn all that, do you?' she said.

'I rather think I do,' I said, though I didn't tell her that it was only the first of many.

At that moment, I felt something round my legs. Looking down, I saw a cat twining its body snake-like around them. Oh heavens, cats!

'Oh,' I said, 'do you have cats?'

'Yes,' said my hostess. 'We have two. Are you fond of cats?'

'Well,' I said, 'yes, I like cats. But I'm afraid I have to keep away from them. I'm allergic to them.'

'Oh dear,' said the woman. 'I'm sorry about that. But we'll just put them out of the room when you're here.'

'Well, yes,' I said, 'but…'

I stopped. I felt dreadful. I'd already asked about a desk and now here I was objecting to their cats.

135

I decided to let it be for the moment. It wasn't their fault after all, as both Mum and I had forgotten to ask whether the people had pets. We almost always did if I was going to stay somewhere, because I didn't just get snuffles but could get a strong allergic reaction. Sometimes it had been so bad that my life had been in danger and I'd had to be hospitalized. Dogs were better than cats, as dogs usually stayed out of bedrooms. Cats explored everywhere. Cats also seemed to make instantly and deliberately for anyone who wanted to keep them away – they'd make a point of jumping onto my lap whenever they could.

I couldn't expect my hostess to understand about asthma and its causes. We'd only learned by experience ourselves. People usually thought it was animal fur that was the problem and that just putting an animal out of a room was enough. But it's not the fur that affects asthmatics – it's the minute and invisible spores that linger on in a room or on a piece of furniture long after the animal has gone. It can take many months or even years before it's free of them. And animals are also not the only causes of asthma, because sufferers can be allergic to almost anything, like me and silk.

We'd discovered about the silk when I was four. In those days there weren't many English children in Helsinki, and the British ambassador and his wife used to invite us all to an annual Children's Christmas Party. That year I was wearing my best party dress – dark blue with a white collar, I still remember – and when I got up from sitting on the embassy's red silk-velvet dining-room chairs, the backs of my legs were covered with a dark rash. Soon after, I was wheezing and gasping for breath. Mum had no idea what was the matter and was terrified.

'It's asthma,' said the ambassador's wife. 'I've seen it before. She must be allergic to something here, though I can't think what. It could be anything. I'm afraid, my dear, you'll have to take her home straight away. She'll probably get better in the car.'

So I was driven home, a bit sorry to leave the party – but at least I'd had the cake. The ambassador's wife had been quite right too – I did get better in the car after ten minutes.

We didn't know then what had caused the asthma, but we later worked out that it was silk. Two or three times in my life I've had asthma very badly because of being exposed to silk – Asian restaurants are a risk, so are weddings and even sitting next to men with silk ties. Horses are very bad too – I can even get asthma if I'm opposite someone on a train who's just been riding. There are also a few other things, but with them the effect takes longer to develop.

So now there were the cats… I didn't want to cause a fuss on my first day with these new people, though, so I just hoped that perhaps this time I wouldn't get an allergic reaction.

I soon made another discovery. My hosts were smokers – and indoors at that. My fault again – I hadn't asked about smoking either. Smoke was something else that could cause asthma and the combination of cats and cigarettes might be pretty lethal. I went to bed but I couldn't get to sleep. What should I do? What could I do? How could I be rude to these people who had so kindly given me a room? They'd never understand properly and they'd think me demanding and ungrateful.

I left early in the morning to get more books and some other things I'd need. Away from my hosts, I rang Mum.

'What shall I do?' I wailed. 'These people have two cats and they're smokers!'

'Heavens!' she said. 'You can never stay there. I forgot to ask Daphne about things like that.'

'So did I,' I said. 'It was just so wonderful to have found somewhere to live.'

'It's a great shame,' said Mum. 'But you really can't stay. It's too great a risk.'

'Maybe it will be OK this time,' I said hopefully.

'That's what you always say, darling. And it's never OK. Do you remember the time when you…'

I cut her off because I knew she was right.

'But what'll I do? It was hard enough to find this room as it was.'

'Didn't you tell me that Barbro had said she'd have you back if you wanted?'

'Yes, she did,' I said. 'D'you think she meant it?'

'Of course she did – she wouldn't have said it otherwise. Ring her up and ask.'

'But what'll I say to my hosts? I feel so guilty.'

'Just tell them the truth – that's all you need to do. I'm sure they'll understand.'

Mum might be sure, but I wasn't. Still, I did ring up Barbro and explain. Would she have me back? She said she'd be delighted.

Even so, I didn't mention it to my hosts that evening. Maybe everything would be all right. Maybe I'd outgrown my asthma stage. Maybe if I took lots of antihistamines as well as my inhaler… But that evening, as I was starting on *The Cell* and making notes in the smoke-filled kitchen, I began to have the tell-tale signs. I felt my chest tightening and a very faint wheeze beginning. I closed my book and fled upstairs to my inhaler. I had to admit to myself that I really couldn't stay. I didn't sleep much again that night as I lay trying to go over the words I would use to my hosts, wondering if they'd be angry. I knew I had to tell them in the morning.

I don't know what I said as I stammered out about the smoking as well as the cats '…and you see, it's no good just putting them out of the room, because it still won't help.

And I really don't have anything against smoking at all – it's just that I can't be with smokers for very long...'

'I'm so, so sorry,' I finally said, feeling terribly embarrassed, fussy and ungrateful. 'It was so kind of you to offer to have me. It's all my fault, of course – I should have asked about the pets and smoking. I didn't remember. I'm so sorry.'

They were very polite and didn't say they minded, but I still felt guilty.

So I packed up once more and took a taxi to Barbro's.

CHAPTER *20*

The day I was due at the Karolinska Institute for our first introductory lectures, I was pretty nervous. I'd kept on trying to decide what to wear, but in the end I went for jeans and a top, because that was what I usually wore and I'd feel more comfortable like that. I knew the intake was about a hundred and sixty students this term and to start with they were not divided into groups but were in one large mass for their lectures. I had to face all that lot, and I knew how people looked at me when they didn't know me, even if I hadn't opened my mouth. They could see there was something odd – wrong – about me. I wished I had a friend there to give me courage – or even an acquaintance. But I knew nobody.

I looked around as we crowded in and finally saw one faintly familiar face. I tried to pin it down. Yes, it was the face of a boy who'd been in the class below me at the Steiner school. I hadn't really known him because although we had spent thirteen years in classrooms next to each other, the Finnish- and Swedish-speaking pupils didn't really speak to each other (I do hope that's something that has changed since my day). The hall for the first lecture was vast, an amphitheatre with row after row of seats. I found the row with the one slightly familiar face and sat down next to him. At least we'd had the shared experience of school and Finland, and he, like me, was a foreigner.

The lectures then and for a day or two were the usual introductory ones: what was expected of us students, what it would be like to study medicine and so on. As I sat or moved around, I could see the usual covert and curious glances from both teachers and students at this odd-girl-out, but nobody said anything. Well, nobody spoke to me at all in fact. But I felt I ought to say something about myself – at least to the authorities. I knew I had got in on paper only and that there had been nothing mentioned about a handicap. I'd learned that the best thing was to face people with the reality at once and get my say in before the usual questions. So now I wanted to tell the staff I knew what I was doing, and that I was quite prepared for the fact that I might find I had to stop in the end. I also wanted to warn them in advance that my handwriting was poor, and that under the stress of exams, it tended to get worse. I didn't think that should matter very much – after all, doctors were well known for their illegible handwriting.

So on the third day after I had started, I went to see the study leader, a woman probably in her late fifties, who was in charge of the introductory course. She listened to me as I said my piece.

'I'm very glad you have come to see me,' she said when I had finished. 'It was of course very good that you got into medical studies.'

Ah! That sounded all right.

'We are very grateful to you in fact,' the woman continued, 'for showing us that there is something wrong with our intake system.'

What? Had I heard what I thought I had?

'You've shown us that we must do something about it,' said the woman, 'so that people like you don't get into medicine in the future.'

She paused, then went on: 'You must understand that medicine is a very tough career. Part of its essence is that patients must accept your expertise and your knowledge, and they need to feel that you know what you are doing. You must realize, Victoria, that they will be frightened of you and that they won't be able to trust you because of your handicap.'

No doubt I looked as astounded as I felt. Whatever I'd expected the study leader to say, it wasn't this. In the far distance echoed all those other voices:

'She may never be able to walk.'

'No, she can't carry that without spilling, can she?'

'You should be in a school for invalids. We don't want you in our school!'

'I'm not letting you go home alone – it isn't safe.'

'They'll never let *you* drive.'

'You'll never be able to be a doctor.'

But nobody before had ever suggested that people would be frightened of me – and as far as I knew, nobody ever had been. Pity I was used to, as well as awkwardness and even slight suspicion – but why on earth should they be frightened of me?

'Now,' said the woman briskly, 'we have a policy in this medical school that if a student leaves in the first two weeks, we then take the next person in line.'

Perhaps she saw my expression, for she changed her tactics.

'You know yourself, Victoria, how hard it is to get in. Think how happy you could make someone else if you gave that person your place!'

She then added, unwisely I think: 'Someone who could really be a doctor at the end of the training.'

She had now got onto familiar ground. The 'you won't be able to manage it' theme. How could she know that? Not yet, anyway. I myself couldn't tell unless I first tried. And not even to be allowed to try? No, I couldn't allow that!

'No,' I said, trying to sound firm, though I felt the tears beginning to rise. (Damn it! Why did I have to cry?) 'I won't do it. I won't give up my place. I've always dreamed of this. I've worked with old people, I've worked with patients who had a very short stay in hospital, and they didn't object to me or distrust me, let alone feel frightened of me. And I'm not going to give up just yet.'

The woman drew breath as if to interrupt, but I went on: 'I know there may come a day when I have to, but that day isn't today.'

Somehow I managed to get up and walk out of the room, tears now choking me. All I wanted to do was to get away and get to the phone in the flat so that I could ring up Mum and tell her about it. I knew she would understand how I felt, and just to hear her voice would be a comfort.

Fortunately Barbro was out and the phone was free. Mum and I spent a long time talking until she finally calmed me down, telling me I had done the right thing.

'They can't make you give up now, can they?' she asked.

'No,' I said. 'I got in and they can't make me leave yet. Not at this stage, anyway.'

'Then that's all right,' she said. 'You'll show 'em.'

'If I fail all my exams, they can,' I said. 'I'm told the drop-out rate is enormous.'

'But that's then,' she said. 'That's for later, darling. You can worry about that when the time comes. Just try and forget what she said. I suppose she meant it for the best – and you know how people are. But she just doesn't know you. So just try and forget.'

Forget? Easier said than done; but I would try.

CHAPTER *21*

And I couldn't really forget. The words about not ever being 'a real doctor' refused to be wiped out. What's more, not a week passed without other teachers coming up to me and asking if I'd really considered properly what I was doing. How could they imagine I hadn't? The idea they harped on about was that even if I managed to pass all the exams and qualify – which they obviously didn't think I'd do – I still wouldn't be able to practise as a doctor. 'Have you,' they asked, 'thought of what you would do if you didn't succeed?' Of course, the result was that I became even more determined to continue. It was like a girl being told by her parents that the man she wants to marry is unsuitable: it usually has just the opposite effect. And anyway, this had been the theme tune of my life so far: 'You won't be able to do it.' And so far they'd all been wrong, hadn't they? So of course I became all the more determined to prove the teachers wrong.

The snag was that I might have got a place to study, but I still had to pass the exams – and they were hard. They were especially hard for me because I'd had no solid background in the type of learning demanded and no training in the type of exam set. It was a bit like my experience at the crammer's in London when I had not known the English system. In that first term, although I passed the oral and written part exams, I failed two out of the three finals. The only one I passed was the first of the two exams in anatomy.

Another worry for me was that I hadn't made any friends yet. I hadn't or couldn't become a part of this large group, and I knew that it often took people some time before they could adjust to my handicap and accept me. Some never could. Perhaps if I'd had a friend then among my fellow students, we could have discussed the exams, how best to prepare for them and to answer them, and I wouldn't have felt quite as desperately lonely and lost as I did. A friend would certainly have saved me money on the endless telephone calls to Mum back in Finland, who mopped up my despairing tears on the other end of the line. Besides, friends had always been tremendously important to me.

There was also another worry at the back of my mind which I couldn't admit to anyone: I was secretly afraid that I wasn't really brainy enough to achieve the demanding level of medical studies. I'd never been confident about my intelligence. At school, others in the class had made it all too clear that there were so many things I couldn't do as well as they did – it didn't occur to me then that these were always physical things – and anyway in our class it had not been 'in' to work. I'd been bitterly disappointed at not getting top results in the matriculation exam, because I'd got it into my head somehow that not to get the best was the same as failure. So inside myself I thought that perhaps I'd just got what I deserved. And then I thought of my brother, who always sailed through his exams with seemingly no problems at all, whereas I always struggled with them. I knew I came from an intelligent family and all my mum's and dad's friends seemed to be the same, but I had this sneaking feeling that I had escaped the winning streak in the gene pool. My mother had tried time and time again to rid me of this idea.

'You know what,' she would say, 'examining at the university has disillusioned me about the reliability of one-off written exams as a test. It's often that a student is simply a 'good 'examinee'. I was one myself and I know what I'm talking about. I could revise and remember anything for about a week before the exam, but afterwards it mostly went out of my head. And I've had students who do so well in their class work and I know they're good, but then somehow in an exam they go to pot and can't show it.'

'But I'm failing so many exams!' I would sob down the phone.

'Listen, darling,' she would say. 'I don't know about you, but I'd much, much rather I had a doctor who could remember what they had learned than someone who learned for an exam and then forgot. Just think of all the chances you're now getting of revising the material and really knowing it forever!'

I couldn't help but laugh through the tears: my mother always did look on the bright side.

'Don't forget,' she'd say, 'life isn't an exam.'

I'd listen and be comforted for a while, but then I would think that it was just my mother being prejudiced in my favour. She also told me that exams were often merely a question of learning and training in exam technique. Although I didn't believe this entirely at the time, I was to prove it had a lot of truth later.

It wasn't just school or exams, though, that made me think I might not be bright enough. There were all those outsiders and strangers, too, everywhere I went, and ever since I could remember, who'd spoken to me slowly and simply, as if I was slow and simple too. I did know really in my head that they were wrong, but I couldn't help but be affected by them.

At the end of my first term, then, there wasn't much to comfort me. Since I hadn't passed two major exams, the rules said that I must take a break. I decided that I would go home to Finland and give my future further deep consideration – that's what they all seemed to want. Nobody at medical school thought I would ever be a doctor. Were they right? I'd finally begun to doubt it myself.

The Swedish system allowed students to take breaks from time to time; in fact as many as they liked and for as long as they liked. I thought this very understanding. Six years of medical studies was a long time, and they came at a crucial period in most people's lives. The average age of the intake at the Karolinska Institute was higher than that of other universities: the maximum age you could apply for medicine there was forty-two and there were lots of people studying who were in their late thirties. I was in fact one of the younger ones. Most of us would get married or find a partner during that time and probably have children as well, but many were already married, often with families as well. They had to find money not only for them but also for studying, the expensive books, living expenses and often accommodation. Many students were forced to work alongside their studies. Crises of various kinds could arise, too: financial, work or family ones. A break of a term or a year or more in one's studies was fairly inevitable. It was even encouraged, and many took the chance. So I too took a break. I was sure my teachers would be very pleased that I seemed to be coming to my senses at last.

I hadn't yet given up, though. Back in Finland I went to work as an assistant nurse at the Aurora Hospital in Helsinki. That way I'd get more experience as well as earn some money. At the same time I was revising for the two exams I'd failed: cell biology and one of the two anatomy exams. In early summer, overweight on the flight in medical textbooks, I joined my mother in north Cornwall, England. She was once more frantically writing a children's textbook there, along with her great friend and co-author, Anne, working to almost daily deadlines. We each sat at our desks in our rooms and worked away, taking time off to clear our heads in the wind and spray of cliff walks. I found it much easier to concentrate when I knew someone else was doing the same. And of course I was not alone.

Perhaps it was the change of scene that helped me to make up my mind about Sweden and to see things more clearly. What had I been thinking of? Of course I would go back! Of course I would give medicine a second chance! Back in Finland, I packed once again for Sweden.

The gap and that decision seemed to change everything. Soon after I got back, I passed both retakes of my exams, so one main reason not to continue was gone. It also showed me that I really could pass tough exams, and so it made me a bit more confident. Secondly, I found myself with two offers of places to live in Stockholm.

I had been perfectly happy living with Barbro, but like anyone else, I really longed for a place which was more my own. Then, too, while I'd been staying there, Barbro had fallen in love with a man and they planned to get married. She'd never been married before, so it came as a bit of a surprise to me – but a very pleasant one because I could see she was so happy. It seemed to me that, as newly-weds, they were hardly going to want a third person around all the time, and that the tactful thing to do would be to get out of their way as swiftly as possible.

The first flat, a student one, had come up at the beginning of the year when I was back in Finland. I'd immediately accepted it – you didn't let such a thing go if your lucky number had come up – but of course I hadn't yet been able to live there. The second wasn't a student flat at all but a studio flat in central Stockholm. It belonged to a friend of Mum's, Brenda Bennett. She and Mum had been co-writing a radio and TV course for adult beginners called *Take it Easy*, which was a co-production by the radio companies of Finland, Sweden, Norway and Belgium. Over the years of shuttling to and fro between Sweden and Finland, Brenda and Mum had become good friends. Brenda was an immensely kind person, and when she'd heard I had nowhere of my own to live, she offered me her flat for the lowest possible rent. It was ideal: the one room was large, it had a high ceiling and an old parquet floor, and there was a small bathroom and a minute kitchen in a cupboard. The big window of the flat overlooked a broad chestnut tree-lined residential side street, and a bus not far away from the entrance to the block went straight to the hospital.

The only doubts I had were because I'd be completely on my own. If I took the student flat, I'd probably make friends more easily and have the comfort of fellow-students around. In the end, though, the choice wasn't that hard – Brenda's flat it was.

Back in Finland, my mother and I piled the vast mass of my clothes, books, files and the paraphernalia of most of my life so far into her car and, hardly able to see out of the windows, we crossed over again on the ferry to Stockholm and installed me in my lovely new flat.

This time of course I was returning and it wasn't all new, but I can't say I wasn't very nervous. There was still the problem of those teachers who didn't believe I should be there; there were friends still to be made, eternal exams to be sat and – worst of all – this second term was the one I most dreaded, because it was the turn of my old enemy chemistry, all fifteen weeks of it, not to speak of the exam at the end.

CHAPTER *22*

I've found that often the thing I'm most afraid of turns out not to be so terrible after all. I even began to enjoy chemistry. I blessed the man who'd taught it to me at the crammer's in London and had made me at least begin to understand it. I took the part exams and they went OK. I left the final until later, because I wanted to make sure that for once I would pass a final first time and not have to resit. So I took it later in August, when I passed it easily. I began to think that I couldn't be so stupid after all.

In this second term the teachers who hadn't met me earlier on always questioned me at some point doing the same lines as before, but my fellow-students had by now accepted me – or at least most remained silent about any doubts they might have. And at last I made friends.

A bit earlier on, I had met a Finn called Jani at a party a friend had given in Helsinki. It turned out he was going over to Stockholm to do medical research, so I had contacted him there. Through Jani, I met a number of his research colleagues, and I now spent a lot of my free time – such as there was – with them. What's more, the one huge group in which we had started as students had now been divided into smaller groups. A small group was always better for me: it was easier for the others in it to get to know me properly, gradually to ignore my handicap, and accept me as one of themselves. A handful of us, a mix of Finnish-speaking and Swedish-speaking Finns plus Swedes, used to study together, and then after the exams we'd go to my flat, where we'd relax by watching TV or a video. I know all this sounds very staid and sober compared with the tales told about the antics of medical students, but, well, I can only say that our studies were so intense that there never seemed any time for the famous 'student life' or for anything much else.

I did do a little baby-sitting, though, as I could also usually study at the same time. I had met an English couple at the Anglican church in Stockholm who had two small children and were invited out quite often. They were delighted to find an English-speaking medical student as a baby-sitter and I was equally delighted to be able to talk – and often moan about my studies – to such a sympathetic couple in our native language. It is odd how comforting free use of one's mother tongue can be when abroad.

Life still had its surprises, though. One evening I was putting my newspapers out for collection in the street outside my little flat when a woman popped her head out of the front door.

'Hello,' she said.

We started chatting and then, very tactfully, she enquired about my handicap.

'Can't the doctors do anything?' she asked, after I had given my usual spiel.

'No,' I said. 'I'm afraid the damage has already been done.'

'Oh,' she said, 'but I'm sure God can do something. Come up to my flat.'

It didn't seem polite to refuse a neighbour. I couldn't imagine what was going to happen. Was she going to read the Bible to me? Were we going to pray?

She opened the door of her flat. Through the hall, I could see into the living-room where a couple of small children were noisily playing some game on the floor. They didn't look up when we came in, and the woman didn't introduce us.

Just inside the hall there was a small stool.

'You can sit on that,' she said.

I obeyed. Then, without warning, out of her mouth poured a loud jumble of sounds.

'Oelksjah flalla-fa-fa ientbtosn sbof otsaaaaah!' she cried.

The sounds seemed to be in no language and were quite incomprehensible. I had heard about people 'speaking in tongues' and could only suppose that this was what she was doing – or thought she was. As the sounds continued, the woman touched my face, my neck and my head. This went on for several minutes – though it seemed much longer. I'm afraid I wasn't a receptive subject, because most of the time I was praying: 'Oh please don't let me burst out laughing.'

All this time, the children took no notice at all of what was happening – no doubt they were used to it.

The sounds and the touching at last stopped, much to my relief. The woman then simply opened the front door again and showed me out. She didn't even say goodbye.

I'm afraid I must have been a grave disappointment to the faith-healer or whatever she was. Later she happened to see me at a petrol station. I was obviously not healed. She didn't speak to me or even acknowledge by a look that the incident had ever taken place. I was one of her failures.

From around that time, though, I was much happier. I still had moments of despair when I failed a test, as I did from time to time, and occasionally a fellow-student or a lecturer would say to me: 'Are you sure you want to go on? You do realize, don't you, Victoria, that you will have to do something else when you're a doctor – not practise clinically, I mean.'

Although this made me angry inside, I did realize that the remarks were kindly meant – just as probably those of my earlier teachers had been. I suppose they sprang from concern that I hadn't taken on board what would be involved. I couldn't really understand why it seemed impossible for some people to accept that I did fully understand but was still determined to prove I could overcome the difficulties. But at least, I thought, they were starting to say 'when' and not 'if'.

It was certainly just as well that I didn't know then that one or more of the teachers had sent a questionnaire to all my fellow-students. The questions were about whether the others thought I should continue my studies, whether they thought I could cope, and if they'd later be prepared to accept me as a colleague. It was only years later that a doctor who'd been in the same year as me referred to the questionnaire. He saw my shock.

'Didn't you know?' he asked.

'I'd no idea till now,' I said. 'Just as well I didn't too. I don't know what that would have done to me.'

'Well, even at the time I didn't think it was… well… fair. I suppose the others didn't either.'

'They certainly didn't tell me, anyway,' I said. 'Perhaps they just threw away the questionnaire – or maybe they even said I was OK. Anyway, full marks to them – and minus marks to whoever it was who sent it round. Do you know who it was?' I couldn't help adding.

'Nope,' he said. 'Don't remember anyway.'

Although I was deeply shocked, I don't suppose that I was all that surprised. There'd been so many things. But I couldn't help thinking about it for a long time and it seemed to me that my fellows had shown much greater understanding, judgement and sheer humanity than whoever had sent it out.

In the spring of 1990 I took another term's break. This time it wasn't because I wanted to consider my future, but the exams I had to pass had begun to pile up and I thought I needed more time to prepare for them. The study system at the Karolinska Institute was that of study points and you had to achieve 220 points to get your degree. This was done by attending courses, each of which gave you a number of study points for the weeks attended. Each course had its own interim exam which, if you passed, meant that you had passed the course. However, you were only awarded the points connected with the course if you passed the final exam on the subject. For instance, say that in term one you did seven weeks of cell biology and thirteen weeks of anatomy, this would give you a total of twenty study points, but only after passing the final exam in each. There were also several 'stop' places along the way, so that for example you could not go on from term one to term two unless you had clocked up at least ten study points. Like many others, I often found myself having taken and passed the courses but without having had time to take the final exams, and so needing to take a break to prepare for them.

After that one term's break, however, I managed to pass all the current missing exams, and so made up a whole eighty of my study points. It was really then that I realized that I did have some kind of a brain after all and could certainly keep up with the others.

The break, though, also meant that I couldn't continue with the group I had been in earlier and had to change to a new one. This of course meant in turn that I had to get to know a new lot of fellow-students and – more importantly – that they had to get to know me. But yet again I managed to make good friends, especially with a girl called Mia. All seemed to be going well, but ahead lay the first experience of actually working in a hospital. I knew this – the clinical experience – was going to be the real test. This was what everyone had said I wouldn't be able to do. Would I? I wasn't that sure myself.

CHAPTER *23*

All of us who'd begun our studies in the same year now had our first chance to practise clinically in a hospital of our choice. The choice was actually not all that free, as it was a lottery system. There were tickets numbered up to 200 and we had to draw tickets in alphabetical order. The higher the number you drew, the less chance there was of getting your first-choice hospital, as all the places there might already have gone to people who had drawn a lower number and so could choose before you. Since my surname began with W, I would be almost the last to draw a ticket. I waited anxiously for my turn. I was lucky – I drew a low number and actually had the choice of any hospital I wanted in the Stockholm area.

There was one snag: I had no idea which hospital would be best for me. My first thoughts always went to my handicap, so now I wondered which hospital would be most prejudiced against me because of it. My experience at the Karolinska Institute had shown me that there was a lot of prejudice around. I could of course have gone to the study adviser for help, but I didn't dare do that because

I was pretty sure that many teachers still didn't believe I could ever do clinical medicine, however many of the theoretical exams I passed. As usual, I rang up Mum for advice. Equally as usual, she was ready to listen.

'Oh darling,' she said as I began to ask for advice, 'I don't think I can possibly advise you. You know you lost me long ago on medical matters – I just don't know enough. But go ahead and tell me about it anyway.'

I outlined the choices.

'Tell me the pros and cons,' she said.

'Well,' I said, 'I don't want to practise at the Karolinska Hospital. I'm certain of that at least.'

'Yes, you would be,' she said.

'And the others – I just don't know. I don't know very much about them. But, well, I thought that maybe Danderyd Hospital might be a possibility.'

'Why there?'

'Mia – you know, my friend – she's going there. That's really the only choice for her as she and her husband live so far in the north of Stockholm. Danderyd is in the north too, so that's the best for her. So I thought if I went there, at least I'd have a friend.'

'Yes, that sounds a very good idea,' said Mum. 'You don't want to have to kick off yet again in a strange place without knowing a soul.'

'Danderyd Hospital is one of the posher ones, Mia says – I mean it has a rather posh catchment area.'

'Does that matter?' asked Mum.

'No, not a bit, I suppose. And I think Mia might be glad to have a friend around as well.'

'Sounds to me as if you've really made your choice,' said Mum, teasing me.

I laughed. 'Well, you know how it is – I knew you couldn't really advise me and that I had to decide for myself, but I just really wanted to hear myself think.'

'Always a good idea,' said Mum.

So I put down Danderyd as my choice. I had no idea at the time that I'd picked the very hospital which, as I was told later – though whether it was true or not, I don't know – was the one with the most prejudice in the Stockholm area. It also turned out to be known for being the toughest place for students practising clinical medicine. They said that if you got through at Danderyd, then you really *were* OK. Doubtful cases were even deliberately placed at Danderyd to test them, so went the rumour. This reputation had somehow passed Mia and me by. Later I thought that the teachers at Karolinska Institute must have breathed a sigh of relief at my choice, thinking: 'That should settle it once and for all!'

I didn't start off well. Just as I was about to begin at Danderyd, my dear godfather John died unexpectedly in England. He'd been a kind of uncle as well as godfather to me all my life, and he was the person who'd given me so much love and support through the gloomy months at the crammer's in London. For me, there was no question of not going to his funeral, so I had to start off at the hospital by asking for three days off to fly to England and back. A godfather wasn't really considered a close relative whose funeral it would be obligatory to attend, but I did all the same manage to get permission from the Danderyd Medical Faculty.

I got back from the funeral in rather an emotional state, and only then began practising under the eyes and comments of the 'real doctors'. These days most people have seen 'hospital soaps' on TV and so have some idea of what happens as medical students go on rounds with the senior doctors, watch as they operate and help diagnose and treat the patients. Daily life at a hospital is mostly without the constant drama of the soaps (and definitely without the complicated personal lives of the staff), but some of them do give a fairly realistic picture of the situation of the medical student. For us it was one of daily pressure, as we were daily being judged, not only by the doctors but by the nurses as well – nurses often see more than the doctor in charge. Naturally, they watched me in particular. I wasn't the usual medical student and at the start they couldn't believe I would possibly be able to do the things expected of me. Surely someone had to have 100 per cent co-ordination to do them? I understood very well how they felt – I was used to it – but knowing I was so carefully watched built up the pressure even more. It also made my cerebral palsy more evident, because my muscles tensed up and my speech became a bit worse.

It was the old story in other ways too. Doctors would start giving the same arguments about my never being able to do clinical medicine – even if they did now seem more ready to believe that I might get through the theoretical exams. People frequently came up to me and asked curiously what I was doing there. Their puzzlement, and sometimes disbelief, when I said I was a medical student was obvious.

There was one unexpected way, though, in which my speech defect came in handy. Danderyd was, as Mia had said, in a posh catchment area and some of the patients had the social snobbery which exists in Sweden as it does in England – since both countries have an aristocratic tradition and an age-old class system. It isn't the same in Finland and I hadn't really come across it there. My Swedish had of course been acquired in Finland, so I spoke Swedish like a Swedish-speaking Finn. There are some Swedes at least who consider Swedish-speaking Finns as 'country cousins' – the original peasants – and therefore socially inferior. So a few of the patients in Danderyd looked down on anyone with a Finnish accent in their Swedish, whoever they were. With me, my speech defect disguised my accent and people thought that any strange intonation or pronunciation was due to that, so they couldn't place me socially. I don't think anyone, patient or staff, had the slightest idea that I was in fact British as well. Though as I'd grown up with 'posh' English, I suppose that might have improved my image.

As the term went on, the pressure mounted. The clinical medicine exam was in two parts: first the practical and then, only if you passed that, the written. This time, you had to pass first go; if you failed, you had to wait another six months before being able to take the exam again, which could seriously delay your already lengthy medical studies.

The day of my practical came. What I had to do was to examine a female patient with the examiner watching me, and to decide what was likely to be her problem. Afterwards, the examining doctor sent the patient out of the room and asked me about her. We talked a little about what I thought was the matter and how I would go about investigating it. After a bit, he said: 'I think you may be wondering whether you have passed or not.'

'Yes, of course,' I said, surprised.

'Well,' he said. 'I don't know what to do.'

All I could do was wait for him to go on.

'The whole time you have been here with us,' he said, 'we've tried to talk to you, tried to make you see that clinical medicine is perhaps not what you should be doing. So I had thought that I would fail you, so that you would have to take half a year's break and think about your options. But...' he paused, '...but after what I have seen you do here, I can't fail you. Go home and read for your written exam on Friday. I'll consult with the others and then we'll telephone you.'

So he hadn't failed me – and he hadn't passed me either. He was going to consult the other doctors and I thought I knew what they'd say. I was desperate to talk to someone at once for advice and sympathy. It was just at this period that Mum, my usual first choice, had gone off to Australia for a conference in Canberra and was going to take three weeks in all on the trip. Although I did ring her a couple of times, she was moving around a lot and those weren't the days of mobile phones or easy and cheap international connections. So instead almost every evening I rang up a friend of the family's in Finland. This was Professor Henry Troupp, who was Finland's leading brain surgeon at the time. His English wife Lotte was my mother's closest friend and I'd known them and their daughters all my life – they were an extension of my family and it was almost automatic to turn to them. Besides, being a doctor, Henry would understand more about the medical situation than anyone else. Despite being a tremendously busy man, sometimes having to operate for nine hours at a time, he always listened patiently to my outpourings. His messages to me could be summed up by: 'Keep at it, girl!' To have Henry believe in me was enormously important and, thanks in large part to him, I had kept at it.

But Henry wasn't in when I rang, nor was my closest friend in Finland, Sussi, so this time I rang my Stockholm friend Jani.

'Just a minute,' he said. I heard some sounds. 'Meet me outside NK in fifteen minutes,' he said, meaning the main department store in Stockholm.

He told me later that he'd been in the middle of an experiment when I rang, but, hearing the tone of my voice, he just abandoned everything, put on his coat and left.

'Now,' he said, when we'd met. 'The first thing to do is to have something to eat.'

'I don't think I could,' I said.

'Well, you may not be hungry,' he said, 'but I am. Besides, it'll do you good.'

It did, but his sympathy and encouragement when I told my story did even more.

'Don't worry,' he said. 'You'll be OK. I'm certain you will. Just read for the exam, because you're going to take it – and pass it.'

After that, he took me out to the cinema. I've no idea what we saw.

Mia, as always, supported me as well. She had passed her clinical exam and now had to read for the written one.

'Now,' she said firmly, 'I'll tell you what we're going to do. I'm going to come to your flat at eight o'clock each morning and go again at five. Before I come and after I go, you can do exactly what you want, but between eight and five you and I are going to study.'

And that was what we did.

Two days before the exam, I was rung up and told that I should go to the Rector of Studies' office at Danderyd Hospital the next day at 4.30 p.m. I'd no idea what to expect, but a summons to the Rector's office didn't sound too good.

When I went in, most of the faculty of the internal medicine section of the hospital were there. They wanted to know why I wanted to become a doctor, and whether I was willing to accept that in medical school there were things I wouldn't be able to do, and that I'd probably have to end my medical studies at some point down the line – perhaps at surgery or gynaecology or something else.

'Are you willing to take this or not?' they asked.

'Yes,' I said firmly, 'I am. I don't have a crystal ball. Nor do you. We'll all just have to wait and see.'

With that, I was allowed to go on to take the written exam the very next day. I can't say the meeting lessened the pressure, though.

It was the first and only time in my life that I sat up all night revising. I just sat reading past exam papers, because

I had at last learned – or learned to accept – the trick of the trade, which was to bone up on past exams.

I passed and was allowed to continue. I imagined my troubles were over.

CHAPTER 24

Our sixth and seventh terms were divided up into subject blocks, each with four weeks of theoretical and four weeks of practical work. My first clinical block was great: it was haematology, problems with the blood, and for once this went without a hitch. The consultant in charge of the ward was very good indeed and didn't seem to have any problems about me at all. Whenever this happened, I always worked better. I enjoyed it hugely.

For the next clinical block, I had to change wards every week. It was during this period that one of the consultants spoke to me and told me I had to come to my senses.

'You've obviously got a brain – you've proved that,' he said. 'It's about time you used it. You must accept the fact that you won't be able to do any clinical work as a doctor.'

I've no idea of the reasons he had for supposing this to be a fact, but I imagined he must have been thinking of patient reaction to me, because his next move was to go to all my patients before I saw them, explaining my handicap. Then he let me go in, examine them and do my doctoring. After this he went back and interviewed them, asking what their opinion was of me. He didn't tell me what they'd said, but I heard that there had then been a meeting of all the consultants about me. It seems that by no means all the doctors had thought as he did, and one there was reported to have said: 'If this girl has got this far, who are we to say she won't become a doctor in the end?' At any rate, the upshot was that once more I was allowed to continue, this time on another ward, thank heavens!

Even so, my self-confidence had once more been deeply undermined. It was never very high at the best of times, anyway.

All those who'd been trying to stop me seemed to assume that it would be impossible for me to practise because patients wouldn't be able to accept me or tolerate me as their doctor. I've no idea how much evidence they had for believing this. I think it's possible it was simply a reflection of their own reactions to my handicap. My own experience with old people and patients before I'd even begun studying medicine had been that some accepted me immediately; a few, after initial doubt or curiosity, then had no problems; and that it was extremely rare for anyone to reject me. My later experience was to be the same. But at the time, I began to have very serious doubts. These were highly experienced doctors, senior figures in the medical world. Were they, after all, right? Had I been kidding myself all this time? Was my handicap so off-putting that patients would have no trust in me? And, if I accepted that, what would I now do and what about my future?

I needed time to think hard about all this and 'to hear myself think' aloud. Mum was yet again in Australia, this time doing research on modern Australian literature and interviewing Australian writers, and I was sure a short call would only worry her. I could of course go back to Finland and talk to people there.

Instead, my late godfather John yet again came to my rescue. In his will he'd left me a small legacy. I had just received it, so I decided to use the money for my summer vacation and to backpack around Australia, ending up by staying with Mum in the flat she had rented in Wollongong in New South Wales. As I also needed a week of external placement in another hospital, I thought I might possibly get a temporary job at the one in Wollongong. I'd really like to have a chance to work in English and to see how English-speaking patients would react to me. While backpacking on the buses, I'd also have lots of time to think about my future.

I rang up Mum to put this plan to her.

'Wonderful idea!' she said. 'That's just exactly what John would have liked you to do with the money. He loved Australia. He'd have been thrilled that you were using the legacy to come here and not for something quite boring. Besides, it means I'll get to see you here. What fun!'

And so it was fixed. I spent five weeks doing the usual backpacker's round, using buses. The times I stopped off at Ayers Rock or Cairns or Brisbane I concentrated on sightseeing, and I didn't want to spoil the experience by thinking about medicine. I left that for the long bus journeys. By the time I reached Wollongong my decisions had ended up as:

- I would continue medicine until I qualified, because at this point they couldn't stop me.
- I'd go back to Finland as soon as I was qualified.
- So as to have a smooth landing in Finland when I returned, I ought to do some part of my studying in Finland to get to know my potential colleagues-to-be.
- Since most people worried about my ability to do surgery (and even I knew I could never be a surgeon – not that I wanted to be one), it seemed sensible to

do my surgical studies in Finland, where I'd have the back-up of home and friends.

- Never, never again would I work a day of my life in Sweden.

Once in Wollongong, I immediately rang up the hospital there. I explained my background and my medical studies so far and they told me to come for an interview. Of course they asked me some questions about my handicap, but it really didn't seem to bother them. They gave me a job for my remaining fortnight as part of a renal team there, working with patients with kidney problems. I was delighted, because I hadn't had much experience of renal work so far, and at the same time it took care of my week's external placement. But how would the Australian staff and patients react to me?

I needn't have worried. The fortnight went far too fast. I had a great time both at the hospital and in Wollongong. Mum and I both loved Australia and the Australians, and much appreciated their kindness, their dry wit and their imaginative way with words. We learned, for instance, that something could be 'as scarce as hen's teeth', that someone having a tantrum was 'spitting the dummy' and to refer to a can of beer as a 'tinnie' and a sausage as a 'snag'. At the hospital I didn't have the slightest problem with either patients or staff. I wondered why not, and thought that maybe it was because I was not these doctors' responsibility, so perhaps my handicap didn't bother them because it was not their problem. It was still so hard to believe that people might simply treat me as they would anyone else.

At the end of my hospital stint, I went to the consultant.

'Can you tell me quite honestly,' I said, 'what you think of my handicap?'

'No problems,' he said cheerily.

'Then what do you think about my future career? Do you think I'll be able to do clinical practice?'

'No worries,' he said. 'I don't see any problems whatsoever. You'll be fine.'

'Do you think you could put that in writing?' I asked. 'You see, I've been having a few difficulties with the doctors in Stockholm. They don't believe I'll be able to be a real one. So I'd be really grateful if you would put it on paper that you think I'm OK.'

'Fine,' he said. 'I'll do that.'

He did it on the spot, too.

I went back to the flat and waved the paper triumphantly at Mum. There were no emails then, of course, but I faxed it from Mum's fax machine to Danderyd Hospital. They should have concrete proof from an English-speaking hospital that I was accepted as a doctor in at least one hospital.

From that moment on, for the two and a half years left, I didn't have any more trouble back in Sweden.

CHAPTER 25

Nor were there any problems when I went to Finland for my surgical studies – with the course, the doctors, or my colleagues. Of course there might be good reasons why it hadn't been the same in Sweden. First, when I came to Finland I'd completed more than half my medical training and had already proved at least something. It could also be possible that back in Sweden some of the Medical Faculty at the Karolinska Institute had early on developed a fixed idea about me and my future which was now ingrained. Another medical school would have no such preconceived idea. That would have gone for Australia too, where the hospital simply watched my work as it was now. It could also be that when studying on my 'home territory' I fitted in better and was thus more acceptable – after all, in Sweden I was always a foreigner. It also made me more relaxed, and I was always better then. Perhaps, too, it was that having the support of home and old friends just gave me more confidence to deal with everything. For whatever reason, it was a great relief.

I also found myself having a student life at last. I became a member of Thorax, the Association of Swedish-speaking

Medical Students, and suddenly there were parties, a night life and also the fun of helping in the annual revue as a make-up artist, including taking the revue to Gothenburg in Sweden. It was such a different and so much happier life that I seriously thought of transferring the rest of my studies in paediatrics and gynaecology to Helsinki. But the stubborn part of me decided to go back to the Karolinska Institute. I said it was to 'give it a chance', but I think it was really because I was determined to prove to them all that I'd made it in the end despite all the forecasts. I'd get my final degree from there and nowhere else. I would show them!

My time in Finland had been well spent, though. I'd gained the confidence there to realize that I didn't have to spend so much of my time in studying as I'd done before, and that I could pass the exams and still have a life as well. I could at last become a real student. Once I was back in Sweden, I became very active in the Association for Finnish Medical Students in Sweden (there were quite a lot of us) and ended up as its chairman. I discovered I very much enjoyed organising things and planning events with others, and that even if it did take up an enormous amount of time, somehow I was able to manage studying as well.

Paediatrics went swimmingly, too, and I was amazed to be given lots of praise by the consultant, which certainly made a change. Then it was the turn of gynaecology. I rang up Mum one day in excitement.

'Mum, Mum, guess what!' I said. 'I've delivered my first baby.'

'Good for you,' she said. 'How did it go?'

'Well, they both survived, if that's what you mean,' I said. 'Mother and baby doing well.'

'I'm sure,' she said. 'But how did you feel?'

'Well, giving birth seemed awfully hard work.'

A laugh came down the line. 'I assure you it is,' said Mum. 'Very.'

'But it was wonderful,' I said. 'When you're dealing with sick people all the time, it's terrific to have a healthy mother and baby and to bring a healthy baby into the world.'

'Might you think of specializing in it?' she asked.

'No, I don't think it's my line,' I said. 'Paediatrics might be, though. But there are the exams to take first.'

'When are they?' she asked.

'Well, I've decided to take the paediatrics one first and the gynae second.'

'And is that the end?' she said.

'Yes,' I said. 'And then it's graduation – for those who pass them.'

'Unbelievable!' she said.

'Cross your fingers when you say that!'

'Oh you will pass, you will.'

I did. The last hurdle was the final oral exam, which I dreaded. In the end, it proved a formality, but I was very nervous, as I always was when I had to speak and so demonstrate my speech defect. I was then furious with myself for not giving the brilliant answers I had so much wanted to do. A last attempt to prove something perhaps.

So finally it was there: Graduation Day from the Karolinska Institute of Medicine. There were a 105 of us, including 40 women. There were two others from Finland besides myself, but only two real foreigners (the other Nordic countries hardly count as really 'foreign' to other Scandinavians). There were all age groups up to 50+, though I was among the youngest, so there were lots of children in the audience waving to their dads and mums and happy doctor dads and mums waving back.

Mum, Johnny and my Finnish godmother Eija had all come over from Finland for it, and I knew they were sitting somewhere in the audience. The ceremony was brief – there were only two speeches, both witty and encouraging. We were reminded in them of what a help being at the Karolinska Institute would be to us in our careers. This was true, as it is the institute that gives the Nobel Prize in Medicine and it is the only one to be really well known outside Scandinavia. I couldn't help it flashing through my mind, though, that to me the Karolinska Institute had also been quite a hindrance. Then I told myself that wasn't fair – it wasn't the Karolinska Institute itself, of course, because it was there that I had got my medical education, and a very good one it was too. By no means every teacher had hindered me, either, and I had eventually made good friends who had supported me and backed me up. It is true that my feelings were and are a bit mixed – I have the Karolinska Institute to thank for having become a doctor at all, but there is a half-buried sting of resentment that some people made it even harder than it should have been. Still, that day, there at my graduation, no sting could spoil my joy. This was a moment I'd been waiting for since I was eleven, and it was at last here. Right now!

We were called up in fives to shake hands and receive our envelopes with our degrees. I looked down at mine. I knew that in fact it didn't contain the degree itself, because there was a reason I'd wanted to delay receiving it officially for a while, but I knew what it would say. Forever after this moment I could write myself as 'Dr Victoria Webster, MD'. I spotted Eija with Johnny and Mum in tears in the audience – we always were an emotional family – and waved the envelope slightly at them. I don't think I listened much to anything after that.

A bit later the Karolinska Institute threw a party and did us proud with sherry, nibbles of smoked salmon, caviar and other goodies. They really made us feel that it was a great occasion, and there was an overall throb of joy, relief and excitement, with everyone, new doctors and their families alike, on a high after the long, hard haul it had been for everyone, not least their supporters.

The rest is a bit of a blur. Johnny and Mum also say they were in such a daze they can hardly remember anything, but we went back to my little flat and had another joyous party with friends from Sweden, Finland and England crowded into my one room, laughing and rejoicing as if I had finally won the lottery. As I had.

It was the end of being a student at medical school and I was indeed a doctor, but it did not mean that I could as yet practise independently. I still had to get a job and do a year more of practical work in hospitals under supervision before I would really qualify. I remembered all too well that it was precisely my ability to practise clinically that had always been questioned. But, as I'd said at Danderyd, 'We'll just have to wait and see.'

CHAPTER *26*

The reason that the envelope I got at the graduation ceremony didn't contain my MD degree was because in my last year I'd applied for a three-month scholarship for further studies at a hospital in the USA. To do this, I still had officially to be a student, so I'd delayed receiving my degree till after I returned from the States.

I'd wanted to go to the States for many reasons. For one thing, I wanted to get more experience; for another, I wanted to go somewhere different before I settled down to a medical career, and an English-speaking country would be easier. I also wanted to see a bit more of the world, especially America. I suppose it was the equivalent of the gap year I'd never had.

I'd been offered places at both Vanderbildt University in Nashville, Tennessee, and at Brown University in Massachusetts. At first I'd thought of Vanderbildt, as it was in a part of the USA that I imagined I might otherwise never see, but then I changed my mind and went to Brown in Rhode Island. My old friend Jani, who'd been in Stockholm, was now doing research at another university reasonably near Brown and, knowing my tendency to homesickness, I thought it'd be comforting to be within reach of a friend.

It was one of my usual frantic departures. Up to the last minute, even while I was packing, I was stuffing application papers into envelopes to go to all the hospitals in Finland that had some kind of vacancy, as I'd still found no proper job for the time when my three months in the States was up. I suddenly remembered I'd forgotten all about currency and Mum rummaged around until she found some emergency dollars I could travel with. As usual, too, I'd packed far too much. However, in the end I got the plane and eventually made my way to Brown.

It was certainly a change of scene. Everyone seemed to use a car to go everywhere – what there was of public transport wasn't considered safe – so one of the first things I had to do was rent a car. Instead of the small family cars I was used to, the one I rented from a firm called Rent-a-Wreck was a silver limousine with red plastic seats. Johnny was very envious when he discovered I was driving a Plymouth. He'd had to work it out, because I hadn't noticed the make, only the amazing amount of petrol it used.

Another surprise, coming from the relative safety of Scandinavia, was to find the hospital heavily guarded. There were security guards with guns on their hips at every entrance and exit, and nobody who worked there, especially a woman, was allowed to leave without being escorted to their car by the guards. The guards then made sure that we could start our cars before they left us. Although I never heard of any problems while I was there, the tight security was probably justified, at least judging by the precautions taken by the tenants of the flat where I eventually lived.

For the first two weeks I'd lived with a cousin of Jani's who was studying medicine at Brown and a bunch of her girlfriends. This was to be only temporary, though, and

I eventually found what I thought was the ideal place: sharing a flat with two male medical students while their third flatmate, Tom, was away. This way I wouldn't be alone but, as they were at the stage of their surgical medical studies where they had twenty-four hours on and twenty-four hours off as a routine, they'd usually be either working or sleeping, so we wouldn't be in each other's way.

When I arrived, I walked into the living-room of their rather big flat, avoiding three bicycles and then tripping over a weight-lifting bench.

'Sorry,' I said.

'Yeah, a nuisance,' said one of the men. 'Have to keep them up here, of course. Can't leave them around. Hi! I'm Joe.'

'And I'm Mark,' said the other.

I looked around. Apart from the bikes and the weights, the most striking thing was that there were big bookcases up against every single window, so that it was impossible to see out. It also shut out the light, of course. Joe saw my puzzlement.

'Looks out front,' he said.

So?

'It's so that we can't see out,' said Mark.

I wondered what this strange American custom might be. He went on.

'The neighbours below,' he said. 'They're drug-dealers.'

'Yeah,' said Joe. 'There's a system, see. If you hear a car drive up and honk, you keep out of the way. You mustn't let them see you – otherwise you'll be in trouble.'

'Not just with the dealers,' said Mark. 'With the buyers, too. They mustn't be able to identify you.'

'Or you them,' said Joe. He pointed a finger at his temple. 'Bang!' he said. 'Got it?'

'Got it,' I said. 'Definitely.'

And I never even tried to look out of the window all the time I was there. I did hear cars drive up and I did hear them hoot and I did imagine a great deal, but I never experienced any trouble myself at all.

After I moved in, the flatmates changed the message on their answering machine so that it said: *This is the residence of Joe, Mark, Tom and Victoria from Sweden.* Mum said it sounded as if I was either a princess or a high-class prostitute.

I spent the first month at the hospital in Casualty. This was again a completely different experience. Casualty was one large room divided by curtains into tiny cubicles, so that when you were working with a patient who was on a trolley you were constantly banging your back or behind into that of the doctor working in the cubicle next door. The first hour of the first day I was greeted by a nurse.

'Hi,' she said. 'Welcome. Here's a suturing kit.' She pressed it into my hands. 'The man behind that curtain has cut himself with a machete. Do what you can to stitch it up.'

'Great!' I thought. I hadn't met a machete wound before, as they don't go in for machetes much in Sweden, but I went off and did what I could. I was to find that in Casualty machete wounds were only a small part of it, and I certainly got the experience I was after.

My next two months after this were in paediatrics and paediatric intensive care, and here it was a different story. There were very few patients, which was a good thing from the point of view of children and parents, but I was very bored and found myself spending most of the time playing patience on the computer.

I was quite lonely too. My flatmates were hardly to be seen and, although I went and had a meal from time to time with Jani's cousin, I never met any of my colleagues properly or was invited out by them, and of course I never went out on my own at night for safety reasons. I spent my free time travelling to see places like New York and in visiting Jani and his girlfriend. I also made a very long journey to go and see an ex-boyfriend in Washington.

Carl was an American doing research in Stockholm when we'd first met. Up to then I'd never had a boyfriend, and I'd sadly come to the conclusion that I might never have one: either they were put off by my handicap or I simply wasn't attractive enough – or both. I didn't have any self-confidence in this respect – perhaps the school experience of people not wanting to touch me had bitten too deep. I was apparently attractive to some people, though, and I used to joke that the only males who fell for me were either six or sixty. Anyway, it had been a huge boost to my morale when a man of my own age became my boyfriend. I was tremendously happy. Carl was only in Sweden for a year, though, and then he'd had to return to the States. We both found that distance did not make the heart grow fonder, and love faded quite quickly into a long-distance friendship. I don't really think either of us had been properly in love – we liked each other, we talked each other's native language, and it was fun having someone to go out with. And I officially had a boyfriend!

In the States, we probably both wondered a little how we'd feel when we met again, but it was fine and later we continued to keep in touch occasionally.

I can't remember having any problems with either patients or colleagues or anyone in the States, though I was conscious of being carefully watched in the hospital at the start to see how I managed. Probably anybody new would have been. I did learn one thing, though, which made me realize I could never practise in the States. Even then, it was a 'suing culture'. At the back of everyone's mind in a hospital was the knowledge that a patient was likely to sue the hospital, the doctor or both if the slightest thing went wrong, real or imagined. This might seem to have its good sides in making everyone extra careful about their diagnoses, actions, prescriptions, operations, etc. The downside, however, is not only the extra stress it puts on staff but also because that may be done unnecessarily because otherwise a doctor or nurse might be accused of having omitted them; or things may not be done because they may have extra risk attached and so carry an extra risk of being sued. As for me, I knew I was a sitting duck for lawyers – my handicap could be blamed for almost anything. So the USA was definitely out as far as my future was concerned.

And what was my future? By the time I left Brown, I'd managed to get a temporary six-week summer job back in Finland, working in the internal medicine department of Mjölbolsta Hospital, about sixty kilometres west of Helsinki. After that, though – nothing.

CHAPTER *27*

When I arrived home in Finland in late June that year, Mum and Johnny were waiting for me with my final certificate from the Karolinska Institute, officially awarding me an MD.

'Doing anything on Saturday?' asked Mum after a while.

'Don't think so,' I said. 'There hasn't been time to fix anything very much.'

'Good,' said Mum. 'I've asked Lotte and Henry round and of course they want to see you.'

'Lovely,' I said. They'd always felt like an aunt and uncle to me – and of course it had been Henry who'd always encouraged me on my bumpy road to medicine.

But on Saturday, it turned out that it wasn't only Lotte and Henry. Mum and Johnny had arranged a big party for all our friends to celebrate my getting my degree. It was one of those wonderful hot Finnish summer days and we all stood around in our sunny garden drinking chilled white wine. Surrounded by all these people, including some of the friends I'd made when studying surgery in Finland, all of whom had wished me well and encouraged me for so many years, I was deeply, gloriously happy.

After they'd all gone, Mum said: 'Oh yes, and there's something to show you.'

She and Johnny took me round to the front of the house.

Johnny said: 'Shut your eyes. And don't look!'

Puzzled but obedient, I shut them. I heard the others move off across the gravel towards the garage. Then they called: 'Open your eyes!'

In the garage shone a silver car, a little Micra. Mum said: 'It's yours.'

'Mine?' I said.

'It's yours. It's your present, darling, for becoming a doctor.'

I couldn't quite believe it. Of course I'd always wanted my own car, but I'd thought I'd have to save up from my salary – if I had one – to buy my own.

'It's not new, of course,' said Mum, 'but it's a pretty good deal. It's only done 4,000 kilometres and it's had just one owner who only used it for shopping.'

'That's just about as good as new,' said Johnny.

'Of course you know I don't believe in giving one's children expensive presents,' said Mum, who had to excuse herself somehow, 'but I thought this was an exception, because you're really going to need a car if you're going to commute to Mjölbolsta Hospital.

'And of course it'll mean there'll only be Johnny to share my car,' she went on. Then she spoilt the effect of not being extravagant by saying: 'Anyway, I always planned to give you your own car if you made it. I knew it was what you longed for. You've deserved it, love, every little inch of it.'

At which point, we both shed tears.

The car's registration number began with FAN, which Swedish-speakers found very funny as it meant 'devil' in Swedish and was a swearword.

So with my little silver devil I travelled back and forth to Mjölbolsta Hospital for the six weeks, hoping by the end to have found a more permanent job at another hospital.

Yet all those applications I'd sent off before I left for the States had not resulted in anything. This was nothing to do with my handicap, as far as I know. The problem was that Finland currently had a surplus of doctors. Something had gone wrong with the plans for the doctor/population ratio and there were currently a great many doctors who were unemployed, especially the new ones. So much so that the Finnish Medical Association and the Unemployment Bureau had set up a course to train doctors who might then be able to get work in the UK. I'd joined this course as an obvious possibility for me. It had consisted of three weeks of training in things a doctor should know about medicine as practised in England, and was then to be followed by a week's trip to London. During the trip the doctors would be taken round various hospitals and hopefully get interviews for posts at them. I'd taken the first part of the course, and was very much looking forward to the week in London, especially as I thought it quite likely, being British, that I might be offered a job there.

Just before we were due to leave, I went to fetch the post. There was a letter for me. I opened it.

'Mum!' I called. 'Guess what! I've been offered a job in the Åland Islands.'

'Åland!' she said. 'Did you apply there?'

'No,' I said. 'At least not recently. I've tried to get summer jobs there a couple of times, but they've always turned me down. The letter's quite out of the blue.'

'So what are they offering you?'

'Two weeks working in Accident and Emergency at the Central Hospital there. It's in the capital, Mariehamn, of course.'

'Two weeks isn't long,' said Mum.

'Better than nothing,' I said. 'And it's in A&E, which I'd like.'

'But what about London then?'

'A bird in the hand…' I said. 'Better than having a gap on my CV. Besides, it might lead to something else. You never know.'

'Do they know about your handicap?' she asked.

'I think so. It said it somewhere in my papers.'

'Well, now they'll be able to see you and how you work. That's good,' she said.

I heard later that the job of Medical Director of Internal Medicine at the Åland Central Hospital had just been taken over by a consultant called Dag Nyman who'd had to find a two-week replacement for a job in the A&E. To save time, he'd simply gone through the previous application papers. I was to find Dag one of the most intelligent people I've ever met and I think that he had perhaps been able to see past the black-and-white words and thought that I was someone who might very well fit into the hospital scene in Åland. At any rate, I got the job. I have to admit there was another reason why I chose to go to Åland, if only for a short period. I'd just started going out with my second boyfriend, who this time was Finnish and working in Helsinki. I was very much in love and thought that the Åland Islands would not be as far away from him as England would be. Looking back, I see that this was one of those turning points in life where two paths open up in front of you and you must choose one, not realizing at the time that the choice will be quite so decisive for your future. As Mum always said: love, whether temporary or permanent, often plays a major part in life's decisions.

So I packed up for a two-week stint in Mariehamn in the Åland Islands, about an hour's flight westwards from Helsinki and quite close to Sweden. As I'd expected, the nurses there on A&E watched everything I did politely but carefully, but I was almost immediately reassured that I wasn't doing so badly. For some reason, the person whose unenviable job it was to make out the work timetable hadn't known that I was a new doctor – and temporary at that – and had only been all too relieved to find he had another doctor on the scene. So I found myself on duty, alone, on the very second evening and night. This was not supposed to happen to a brand-new junior doctor, and it was a pretty scary experience. Two senior doctors, one of whom was my official back-up and on call if I needed help, were dining out together that evening. When they realized I was alone, they returned to the hospital and crept into the A&E department. I was busy working with a patient.

'What are you doing here?' said the night nurse. 'You're supposed to be off duty, aren't you?'

'Is everything all right?' they asked the nurses. 'How's the new girl doing?'

'Fine. You go on home,' they said, shooing them out of the door. 'Victoria's doing fine. No need for you.'

And fortunately that night there wasn't.

After two weeks the hospital offered me a real job, starting the following January. I accepted with joy and relief. My boyfriend and I took two weeks' holiday and went to stay in Mum's house in Cornwall. It was a small cottage in a fishing village where there were glorious hilly coastal walks all around. We had just returned from one of these when the telephone rang. It was from the hospital in Mariehamn.

'We're in a bit of a spot,' said the doctor. 'Can you start earlier?'

'When?' I asked.

'In the middle of December,' he said.

That was a bit of a shock, as it was very soon, but you don't turn down such a request when it's your first job.

'Well, I'm in England at the moment,' I said, 'but I think I'll be able to make it.'

'Good,' he said. 'See you then.'

CHAPTER *28*

I didn't know much about Åland before I went there, except where it was on the map and that it was mainly Swedish-speaking. I'd once been there in the summer, cycling for a week, so I knew the islands were closer to Sweden than they were to Finland, much in the same way as the Channel Islands are closer to France than they are to England. There were only about 10,000 people in Mariehamn, where the Central Hospital was, but of course there were many more in summer, when the tourists came. The Central Hospital served the whole of Åland, including all those living on the thousands of outlying islands which can only be reached by boat or, if in a critical condition, by helicopter. It took about five hours by ferry to get to the furthest one of all.

It was in so many ways the perfect place for me to start my career: a small population, a small hospital and a small staff. Unlike other hospitals I've since worked in, the head doctors and the junior doctors met twice a day for coffee, so that everyone got to know each other and we were able to discuss problems together.

Soon after I arrived I had a call from one of Åland's two small daily papers.

'We'd like to have an interview with you,' said the journalist at the other end.

'With me?' I said. 'Why?'

'Well, you're a new doctor for Åland. And we've heard quite a lot about you.'

Oh yes, I thought, it's my handicap. That's always newsworthy. But well, why not? I'd had a growing feeling inside me ever since I had become a doctor that my career might be encouraging to those who had a handicap and to their parents. After all, I knew all too well what prejudice there was, and I thought I might be able to encourage somebody else to chase their dream despite all those people saying they'd never be able to do it. So I said yes.

'And of course we'd like to take some photographs,' said the journalist.

Oh God, photos! I hated seeing myself in photos. I always tensed up and my spasticity showed. When I saw my face in a mirror I wasn't nervous and it seemed quite normal, but when I saw it in a photo looking lop-sided and awkward, I could hardly bear it. Of course newspapers always wanted photos. I'd just have to go along with it and not look at the results.

I then worried the night before about what I would say, what I should wear, if it'd be OK, and a thousand and one other things. I did make sure to ask, though, if I could read the article through beforehand and change anything I didn't want in. It turned out fine, and the journalist and I got on very well. The photo wasn't all that bad either – because of course I couldn't stop myself looking at it after all.

The interview turned out to be a very sensible thing to do anyway. It meant that most patients already knew about me when they came to the hospital, and I didn't have to explain so much before I saw them. I'd already begun to realize that a brief explanation at the start about my handicap made it easier for patients to accept me as their doctor. The other major reason for acceptance was the miracle of the white coat: put on a white coat, hang a stethoscope round your neck, and you're a doctor! I knew this from watching TV thrillers, where it's a trick much used by villains – and some heroes – to get access to hospital wards, but it's also true in real life.

People of course soon forgot the newspaper article, but by that time I'd usually treated a patient's friend, uncle or second cousin twice removed, so they'd heard about me. Åland is that sort of place. In fact I never went into a supermarket in Mariehamn without bumping into a nurse, a colleague or a patient. The patients or their relatives would usually recognize me before I did them, so it became a memory-hunt for me to discover what their problem had been.

'Knee getting on all right, is it?'

'How's your daughter doing?'

Or then the capitulation of: 'Sorry, I can't quite remember what the problem was. Remind me.'

But I mostly did remember, because it was important to them that I did. No, Åland Central Hospital was certainly not an impersonal, faceless repair factory.

Another way I got to know a lot of people was being heavily involved in the Scouts. I'd been active earlier in Helsinki, too, where I'd made life-long friends among them. When I was grown up, I'd also become a leader on various camps. In the Åland Islands I became a leader for the Sea Scouts, which was also fun. Through the children, I met the parents, so that was another way people got to know me and about me. It was a hard fact that was always to be true that once people knew me as a person, they lost their wariness, suspicions, distaste, fear or whatever it is that a handicap provokes.

My time at the hospital was not only spent in A&E and at that time I hadn't yet made up my mind what I wished to specialize in. Although there is a specialty in General Medicine in Finland, the system doesn't work quite like the GP system in the UK, and doctors mostly specialize in some particular aspect of medicine. I was a very junior doctor, doing my first proper job, and the rules said that I first had to do a year under supervision before I could become a licensed doctor allowed to practise on my own. This also meant I could try out working in different areas to see a little of what each was like before I chose my specialty. The training was purely practical – you simply did the job, but under a senior doctor. So I was at times on the internal medicine ward, the surgery ward, the children's one, and so on. The internal medicine ward work I did was terrifying, as I was almost always on it alone even though my senior could be called, so I had to decide myself about each patient. 'Internal' is a wide term and we had to deal with a great variety of cases, so I found myself with patients with cancers of all kinds, some with infections of the skin, lungs, urinary tract, etc., others with diabetes, or with angina and other heart problems, as well as a wide variety of intestinal cases. It was certainly a challenge, to say the least. I did, though, have a colleague, Clara, who realized how tough I was finding all this and would regularly pop her head round the door to check that I was coping. She was a great comfort.

As for the surgery ward, well, I knew that with the very fine co-ordination that surgeons need, I would never be a surgeon. Even if I had wanted to be, that is, because surgery is very much hands-on while doing an operation, but outside that a surgeon's dealings with the patients are limited. I much preferred the clinical side of medicine and interacting with patients and with their relatives.

I had a spell on the paediatric ward as well, which I thought might become my area, not only because I liked children but because they usually took to me, too. Children were mostly unhampered by any preconceived attitudes about handicaps. I suppose young children meet with so many new things daily and with so many new people of different ages, appearances, heights and so on that they have no norm for a time – unless, of course, some kind of prejudice has already been instilled into them. To them, a doctor is a doctor – why should she not have a handicap too?

I began to realize that I did not really enjoy ward work – there was too little clinical medicine. The only real clinical work was between 9 a.m. and 11 a.m. when you did your ward round. That was the time you saw your patients and treated them. The rest of the time the doctors for the wards were doing paperwork: admitting people to the hospital, writing up their reports, writing prescriptions and filling in the forms for sick leave and other matters. I was always in a hurry and there was just never time, ever, to do it all. So I would work from 8 a.m. to 7 p.m. most days, though on some of those I was on call for A&E as well.

A&E, on the other hand, was intensely clinical and immensely varied. The hospital in Mariehamn was the only hospital for the whole of the Åland Islands, and so it dealt with everything. As a doctor there, I had to decide what was the matter with the patient and then exactly how ill he or she was, usually without a senior to help in the decision – although they'd be on call, so could be reached by phone and give me advice. I had to interpret X-rays, suture wounds big and small, do lumbar and knee punctures, set fractures, treat infections and burns, diagnose strokes and heart problems, deal with home accidents, muggings (a few), drug abuse, head injuries, car accidents and – because of the sea all around – treat hypothermia and near-drownings. I had also to make a decision after a phone call as to whether a patient on one of the remote islands needed helicopter transport or not. Sometimes, too, a decision had to be made about whether a patient would be better treated at the bigger hospital in Turku on the mainland, as Mariehamn might not have the resources to deal with the problem.

The patients were varied too, young and old, men, women and children. In the winter they'd mostly be the Swedish-speaking Ålanders, but in the summer the tourists came to visit in their thousands for their holidays. They often travelled on the large ferries, almost like luxury cruise ships, which ran several times a day between Sweden and Finland or Estonia. As these mostly stopped in Mariehamn, the patients could be people from all countries and speaking many languages. Especially here it was useful that I was trilingual; I had also learned German at school, even if I was very bad at it. The ships' call in at Mariehamn was not strictly speaking necessary for the journey, as it was a detour, but in another way it was essential for the survival of the shipping companies. The tax-free regulations made short trips very popular with both Swedes and mainland Finns, and from Åland's point of view the ships were an important source of harbour dues and income, as well as the tourist trade. For us, they were a source of patients.

Åland, however, is a peaceful place, and in all the time I was there I never had to treat a gun wound or a knifing. We had a number of chainsaw and axe wounds, though: one patient of mine succeeded in chopping off half his leg with an axe. And of course sometimes a road accident could end in horrific injuries.

My family continued to be amazed that I seemed to enjoy and want to do this work.

'How can you stand all that blood?' they would ask.

'But you're such an emotional person. I mean, you cry at the drop of a hat. How do you bear it?'

'How can you stand it? All that – sick children, their parents, the elderly… seeing the pain?'

Well, it's true that I am an emotional person in my private life, but work is something else again. From day one at medical school you learn that however much empathy you may have with patients, when you are on the job you aren't yourself but 'someone doing the job'. You learn to put a professional shield between yourself and the patients. You have to, or you couldn't deal with it. Each course at medical school causes your empathy to diminish – that's a proven fact – and it's drilled into you to accept that this is a profession, nothing personal. 'Drilled', yes – I imagine it must be a bit like being in the army, where surely it must be instilled into you that you're doing a job, and that you must distance the person that is you from your acts. Otherwise how could you cope with destroying, maiming and killing? Mind you, it would be a sad day if a doctor simply became a machine, and I'd like to think that a patient would never become to me a body in a bed and not a person.

Another question Mum asked me was about death.

'What about when people have something terminal? Or when they do die? Isn't it awful having to tell the relatives?' she asked.

'Yes,' I said. 'There's that too. The first patient to die on me, so to speak, happened very early on. It upset me very much. Even though the death was inevitable, I went over and over it in my mind, wondering if there was anything at all I could have done. There wasn't – but that's what you do. And it was very, very hard to tell the relatives, and difficult not to become emotional myself. Because of course I put myself in their place and remembered learning of Daddy's death. But as time's gone on, I've become more professional at that too.'

'How do you approach it?' she asked.

'Well,' I said, 'you learn to sum up the relatives as to how they will take it and to adapt the way you tell them. I find telling them that there has to be an autopsy is one of the hardest things. You can imagine how some people react to the idea. But it often has to happen when the death is outside the hospital.'

'Yes,' said Mum. 'I hated the thought when there had to be an autopsy on Daddy.'

'But you said yes,' I said. 'Some next-of-kin can say "Absolutely no way" and then I somehow have to persuade them that it's something that must be done.'

'Do you get a professional shield about that too?' asked Mum.

'Well, yes,' I said. 'Of course. But all the same I hope I never get totally used to it or blasé about it. It's a fine line to tread.'

And actually, in these respects I began to find that my handicap could sometimes be a strange asset with patients and their relatives. Some found it much easier to talk to me than to a 'perfect' doctor. They even said this. They explained that it was more comforting to think that their doctor had also had problems and would maybe therefore understand them better. Often a doctor in a white coat would seem to them like a being from another world, like an alien god pronouncing on life and death who had not experienced hardships or suffering in the real world themselves. Nonsense in reality of course. They also sometimes said that they could understand me better because I spoke slowly and didn't gabble out my words – I must say that was a spin-off from my speech defect I certainly hadn't thought of before.

It was working on call on A&E that made me realize in the end that I'd perhaps found the job I wanted to do. I liked the action, dealing with people and their relatives all the time, and above all I enjoyed the variety of clinical work and the need to diagnose correctly and start your patients on the path they would then follow in the hospital. The head of A&E in Åland was now a doctor in his late forties called Jan Österberg. He was someone who was very kind and considerate to his patients and colleagues, and he had a sense of humour more like that of a Brit than a Finn, which was something I much enjoyed. I was lucky to have him as my first boss, and I know I was considerably influenced by him, his work and the truth of his axiom: 'The A&E doctor is the patient's advocate within the healthcare system.'

I felt I too wanted to be the patient's advocate and to make this my specialty.

There was one big hitch, however. A&E was not a recognized specialty in either Finland or Sweden at that time. To be a senior doctor working on A&E in these countries you had to have specialized in internal medicine, surgery or anaesthesiology, but there was no special training for the work on A&E such as there was in countries like the USA, France and England. Yes, there was England. Obviously, as a British subject, the thing for me to do would surely be to go to England and try to get my specialty there.

I thought about it for a long time, lying awake for many nights. Finally, I went to Jan and explained what I wanted to do.

'You want to go to England?' he said.

'It's not because I'm not happy here,' I said quickly. 'I am. But I think I want to work in A&E permanently, and I know there won't be a slot here for a long time, will there.'

'No,' he agreed, 'there probably won't.'

'And I still want to make sure it really is my field. I think that to find out I need to work in a much bigger hospital.'

'Yes, I can see that,' he said. 'But why England? Oh, I suppose it is your native country – I always forget!'

'Most people do,' I said. 'And besides I belong to Finland, too. But it's not just that – I know that A&E is a specialty in England and perhaps – just perhaps – I might be able to get that there. It'd be really great if I could.'

I don't know what Jan thought of that idea, but anyway he said that he'd try and help me and would give me a reference and the names of some contacts.

So I wrote off to three or four. Only one replied – from Edinburgh – so I went there to have an interview with the consultant in A&E, a man called Tom Beattie.

What I hadn't told Jan was that I had another motive for going to a big hospital. One of the reasons I was happy in Åland was because I was so accepted as a doctor there. I felt this was largely because I was well known in a small community. In another hospital, A&E would be an area where you saw new people all the time – what would happen to me when I was in a big-city hospital where I could not possibly be known to the majority of patients or their relatives, or even to many colleagues? At the back of my mind there always lurked those echoes: 'Remember, patients will never accept you as their doctor or learn to trust you.' Had I been lulled into a false sense of security in tiny Åland? Would I be accepted elsewhere?

I had to put it to the test. I just had to know.

CHAPTER *29*

It was a glorious sunny day in Edinburgh. I was nervous as I walked to the hospital for the interview, but Edinburgh was a comforting place for me: my father had worked there before he came to Finland. I'd only visited it once before for a few days, but I felt it was part of me in some odd way.

I liked Tom Beattie at once and we talked for a long time. He asked me the usual questions – about my background, my reasons for wanting to come to Britain and to do A&E, and of course about my handicap. I gave him the usual answers. Then he said: 'Why are you interested in Edinburgh?'

I didn't like to say that he was the only person who had answered my letter, so I told him about my father and that he'd grown up in Elgin and later taught at Edinburgh University.

'Have you got relatives here then?' he asked.

'No,' I said. 'I'm afraid all his close family are dead.'

'Friends?' he asked.

'No, I don't know anyone here. I've got lots of family and friends in the south of England, but I'm afraid I don't know anyone at all in Scotland.'

'Where in the south?' he asked.

'In and around London,' I said. 'And then in the south-west. My mother's got a little house in Cornwall we go to – and then I've got cousins and friends in Somerset and Devon.'

'Well, Edinburgh would certainly be a long way away from all of them,' he said.

After a few more questions, he said: 'You know A&E is a very, very tough specialty.'

'Yes, I know.'

'You'd probably find it a lot tougher in Britain than in Finland. Your present hospital is rather small by the sound of it.'

I told him that was one of the points about coming to the UK: I wanted to experience working in a bigger hospital.

'Yes,' he said. 'I understand that. But you're likely to have to take a step down in a British hospital from what I gather your position is now. It's equivalent to a British registrar, isn't it?'

'Yes, just about,' I said.

'Well, here you'd be one below that – a senior house officer.'

'I did realize that,' I said, 'but I still want to do it.'

'How many hours a week do you work in Finland at the moment?'

'The regulation hours are thirty-seven,' I said, 'but with nights as well it probably comes to about fifty or so.'

Tom Beattie grimaced. 'Here it'll probably be more like seventy-two. I know those are truly dreadful hours, but that's the way it is at the moment. Both junior and senior house officers in A&E here are under terrific pressure all the time.'

Seventy-two hours did sound pretty awful, but I told him that I wanted to try all the same.

'The trouble is that working as much as that you'd need support when you were off duty. You'd need the support of relatives and good friends right from the start. And here in Edinburgh you wouldn't have it.'

It sounded to me as if the support would be needed at work as well as off duty. But of course I was used to people trying to tell me I couldn't do things. Was that what he was doing?

'Have you thought of applying to Derriford Hospital in Plymouth?' he asked after a moment.

Plymouth? Derriford? No, it hadn't crossed my mind.

'You said the south-west of England was where you had family and friends. That's where you should be going, not here. And Derriford would certainly have a big enough A&E for you – it's the biggest in the south-west of Britain.'

My disappointment must have shown.

'I'll give you a couple of names to write to at Derriford,' he said. 'I know them both. Send off an application. And the best of luck.'

Somehow I trusted Tom Beattie. I didn't think he was put off by my handicap, or didn't want me at his hospital and so was trying to palm the problem off onto someone else. I felt he genuinely wanted to help and was advising me for my own good. I wrote off to Derriford.

It was perhaps lucky I didn't know there were about 200 other applicants for the job that was going, which was initially for six months in the A&E department. I had two interviews, one with a man called Henry Guly, who was in charge of the whole department, and one with Iain Grant, who was in charge of the senior house officers. I actually enjoyed the interviews – I don't think I've ever laughed so much during an interview as I did then – so I was rather optimistic when I returned home.

But then the weeks went by and I heard nothing. My optimism fled. I was glad to be doing a temporary job in the meantime at Lohja Hospital, which was not too far away from Helsinki. The job was in anaesthetics, as I'd realized I needed some different anaesthetic experience than what I'd had in Åland. There weren't any problems with my handicap – everyone seemed to accept it – though I did find it sad and depressing when every day my morning task was to put to sleep girls and women who were in for an abortion.

And then, finally, I heard from Derriford. I was in!

'Great!' said Mum. 'When do you start?'

'In January sometime,' I said.

'How'll you go?' she asked.

Of course I hadn't begun to think of the details, as I always tended to put this sort of thing off.

'And where will you live?'

'I think on the hospital campus to start with,' I said, 'but then I'll have to find somewhere else of my own. A flat somewhere, I suppose.'

We thought about this. Neither of us knew Plymouth itself at all. How hard was it to find places to rent? What did they cost? Our little house in Cornwall was only about one and a half hours' drive away, but you couldn't commute from there if you worked in A&E, because obviously you had to be near the hospital. Besides, commuting would have been far too exhausting with the hours we had to work.

We used to joke that we were a family of organizers, and sure enough we were soon planning.

'You'll need a lot of things, won't you,' Mum said. 'If you're planning to stay on for a year or two, that is.' I was.

'We'll just have to go to England by car, don't you think? You'll never be able to travel light.'

I laughed – I never could.

'I tell you what,' she said. 'I've got a General Synod meeting in February, if you remember.'

Mum had fairly recently been elected as a lay representative for the Diocese in Europe on the General Synod of the Church of England. In fact she ended up as a

199

chairman of the whole thing. It met twice a year in London and in York, but she seemed to have many more meetings than that.

'So...?' I said.

'Well, why don't we drive down together via France, stop for a couple of days in Paris, and then cross to England? We'll be able to share the driving and it would be fun.'

'Great idea!' I said. 'Then I can just throw my stuff into the car.'

'And I could throw in my huge pile of reading stuff for the Synod. It weighs kilos!' said Mum. 'What about us going to Cornwall first and then to the hospital?'

'And maybe you'd like to help me find a flat,' I said. 'I'm never going to have time to look.'

'Oh, I'd love to!' she said. 'You know I like house-hunting.'

So that's what we planned.

It was when we were throwing my stuff into the back of the car the day before we were due to leave that Mum stepped into a puddle outside our front door. Only there turned out to be ice at the bottom of it. She slipped and cracked her thighbone. In no time at all I was back in an A&E department in Finland, this time with Mum, and that was the end of that plan.

The delay was in one way a good thing, because almost every day after being accepted I got a new letter from the hospital asking for a new document before they could employ me. Separately – never simultaneously – I got asked for a certificate to say I hadn't got hepatitis B, my CV in Swedish, my CV in English, the curriculum of my studies at the Karolinska Institute, my certificates from there and references from two doctors. When I got a request for this last one, I rang up Derriford to say that they'd had all of these papers nine months before.

'Sorry,' the woman said. 'They've never been passed on to us and we need them for the official records.'

I sighed. 'OK,' I said. 'I'll send you copies again. But I'd like to ask you one or two things about the job now.'

'Sorry,' said the woman again. 'I can't do that. You see, we aren't allowed to give you any information about the job until we've had your papers.'

It sounded screwy to me, but I presumed they had their reasons. Cursing bureaucracy, I sent them what they wanted all over again, supposing that now I'd finished.

A short while later, I attended the annual 'Doctors' Days' in Helsinki, where I happened to chat to a visiting English doctor. I told him I was going to work in Derriford Hospital.

'Have you registered with the General Medical Council in England?' he asked.

'No,' I said. 'I didn't know I had to. Derriford never mentioned it.'

'Good heavens, yes!' he said. 'You've got to be legally registered with the GMC before you can work as a doctor in Britain. You'd better contact them right away. They're going to want lots of papers.'

They did. I had to have umpteen more certificates from both the Swedish and Finnish authorities plus, lastly, they wanted my passport. Not just a copy of it, mind you, but the original. And of course, I was due to travel very soon and would need it.

I went to the British Embassy in Helsinki. They were horrified.

'But you can't send it!' said the woman at the consulate. 'It's illegal to post a British passport from abroad.'

Well, I could see the sense of that. Things disappear in the post, registered or not, and passports must be extra desirable.

'What am I to do?' I asked.

'I can give you an official document instead to certify your British nationality,' the woman offered.

I rang up the General Medical Council. No, they said, that wouldn't do – they had to have the original passport. When I told them it was illegal to post one, they said they did it all the time. I let that go, but tried another tack.

'I've got to travel in a week to take up the job, and I have to carry my passport to get out of Finland and into England.'

After much argument, we agreed that I would post it the moment I set foot in England, which would now be six days before I began work.

So, once more I was packing, this time to go on a plane. Somewhere around midnight still found me as usual crouched over my cases, trying to unload some of the less essential items, rather like lightening a ship so that it wouldn't sink. Even so, I had to pay vast sums for excess baggage. But at least I was off, with a by now familiar mix of excitement and trepidation.

I was on my own once more.

CHAPTER 30

I'd been to the UK every year since I was born and sometimes more than once. We'd mostly been visiting our many friends and relatives there in the holidays. But that wasn't to say that I knew it very well. The only big city I knew at all was London, where I'd lived for the four months or so when I was at the crammer's. The other bits I knew were in the south and the south-west, especially Cornwall. So when I arrived, Plymouth seemed a very big city to me, and its main hospital, Derriford, a very big hospital.

It was really huge – at that time it had over 1,000 beds – and its catchment area was very large. Plymouth itself had a wide social spread, including one of the poorest districts in Europe with a great number of illiterates. It also had a sizeable Hispanic population who sometimes didn't speak much English. It was also an important port, so it had a dock area, and a naval base with naval personnel. This meant there were naval medical staff at the hospital as well as the usual civilian staff. What's more, it was a trauma centre for the whole of the south-west and so covered a lot of cases from Devon and Cornwall, which both had many agricultural and fishing communities. Add to this the usual city population and its problems and you have an immense variety of people and cases.

We saw about 300 patients in any twenty-four hours, whereas in Åland it had been about twenty per day in the winter and forty to sixty in the summer. Not unexpectedly, there were many more crime-related and drug-related cases in Derriford, as well as sadly many more cases of abuse, both of adults and of children. There were also several types of illnesses and injuries that I hadn't come across before. If I'd come partly for greater experience, I was certainly going to get it. If I'd come to see whether patients of all kinds who had never set eyes on me before would accept me as their doctor, I'd also come to the right place.

My first week was a tremendous medical culture shock. So very many things were different from my hospital experiences in Finland and Sweden, both for good and bad. I hadn't foreseen one problem, though – the language. English was my native language and in ordinary life there'd never been any problem at all. But I hadn't thought about the fact that I'd trained for medicine in Swedish and practised in Finnish and Swedish, but so far I'd hardly any experience at all of practising in English. I found myself groping for medical words that I'd never come across before. This rather baffled my colleagues, who mostly had no idea of my background, and it must have made me come across as knowing a lot less than I did. Perhaps it didn't matter at the start, though, as I'd taken what amounted to a demotion in my status, just as Tom Beattie had predicted. In Derriford I would be an SHO, a senior house officer, one step above a junior doctor, a JHO, and one below a registrar.

The medical training in England was a different system to the one I'd been through in Sweden, where clinical practice was built into the basic training. Here it came later and so the group of medics into which I had been put seemed to me to be at a very early stage: the first of our training sessions had been on how to put in stitches. We were told that we couldn't put a single stitch into a patient until our stitchery had been 'approved'. I'd been stitching up patients for the last four years – and only the previous day in Derriford I'd put five stitches in a patient and then sent him home, as it hadn't even occurred to me that I was not allowed to do it. The next session we practised intubation – putting a tube down a patient's throat – on dolls. The doctor teaching us came over and watched me, saying at the end: 'Wow! You did that well!'

I just couldn't be bothered to explain that I'd already been doing it on people, let alone dolls. I decided to sit back and enjoy the new experience of being top of the class. Of course, the usual suspicion inside me was that people were surprised I could do anything at all with my handicap; on the other hand, there was always the possibility in England that the reason for their surprise could be because I'd had a suspect 'foreign' training and not a British one. I'd long ago discovered that most countries believe their own education to be streets ahead of any other. Still, it was all rather frustrating at the start, as I'd come to Derriford to learn new things.

In another way, very many things were new. For one thing, so much was done differently. Some of the things I'd been doing for the last four years were here considered 'old-fashioned' and 'not evidence-based'. So in a way I was thankful that I was an SHO and had to go back almost to square one. What with that and all the English terminology, I was also very glad that I had decided not to take my first crack at Part I of the MRCP exam (to become a Member of the Royal College of Physicians) until after six months.

One of the other differences was in what SHOs were allowed to do. In Finland, when after a year you became a licensed doctor and were allowed to work independently, you were left to get on with it on your own, without a senior monitoring you all the time. In fact, seniors in Finland don't really know very much about what their juniors do, even if they are on call as a back-up. As one of my seniors, Dag Nyman, had said in Finland: 'The problem is that juniors tend to ring about the wrong patients – the ones they admit. I can always see those the next day. It's the ones they send home without my knowledge I worry about.'

In Derriford, we always had to talk to a senior for the first weeks about all our patients before we were allowed to deal with them on our own, whereas that was what we had done as part of our training in Sweden. With me, it was fortunately after only about three weeks in Derriford that someone came up to me and casually said: 'Oh, by the way, you don't have to talk to a senior any more before you send a patient home.'

Which system is best? It's hard to say. Of course it's important at the start to see that new doctors in a hospital are competent to handle things themselves; on the other hand, juniors don't develop much confidence in their own judgement if they always have to consult a senior. It can also happen that a junior who may be tired (or just lazy) doesn't bother very much if a senior is going to make the decision anyway.

Then there were the notes. In Finland and Sweden all notes the doctor made about the patient had been first dictated, then typed up, and finally kept permanently among the patient's other papers. A doctor could always look them up easily. In Derriford A&E department, however, the notes were all handwritten; they were only kept for a year and then destroyed. These handwritten notes were frequently illegible – I'm sure mine were – so it made it difficult to follow up the patient even within that first year. After a year it was impossible anyway. I found this system made things much more difficult and wasted a lot of time, because you had to start at square one with your diagnosis and couldn't build upon a previous doctor's diagnosis and treatment. Later on, I was to realize this had its good sides as well, as a doctor could not then be over-influenced by a former opinion or decision.

But perhaps the difference that struck me most was in hygiene, not so much in the hospital building itself as in the clothes of the doctors and nurses. The dress code was very strict – much stricter than it was in Scandinavia. The male doctors had to wear a tie at all times and a clean, well-pressed shirt. One day, to my astonishment, I heard my usually relaxed consultant ticking off a junior doctor for having a crumpled shirt. The female doctors mainly wore skirts or then proper trousers – no blue jeans were allowed. I managed to get away with wearing coloured jeans, a distinction which I found comic. I just about never wore skirts and the day I did so, a colleague commented: 'Ah! Dr Webster has legs, I see.'

'Mm,' I said. 'For what they're worth.'

But it wasn't so much the more formal dress for doctors that struck me – it was that doctors didn't wear white coats or any protective clothing over their clothes. With the men, this meant that their ties were always getting in the way. When I saw a male doctor bending over patients in their hospital beds, I could see the tie drop down on the patient and the bed and then the doctor move on to the next patient, where the same thing would happen.

'Not good for hygiene,' I'd think. 'All that risk of cross-infection.' But I didn't say anything.

And then doctors – including me – went home in the very same clothes they'd been wearing all day. If they'd been wearing suits, the men probably also wore them for many days and weeks as well. I was glad to hear that things later changed and the medical staff do wear scrubs nowadays. It probably took the start of the MRSA scare in England to make a change.

The nurses did have to wear uniforms, however, and the type and colour depended on their seniority. The snag about hygiene here was that the nurses had to wash the uniforms themselves at home, so they came to work in them, spent the day in the hospital in them, and then went back home in them, often doing the shopping on the way. It was a mystery to me that nobody had ever thought of all the health hazards involved.

Another difference was the patients' nightwear in Derriford. In the hospitals I'd been in before, hospital nightwear, dressing-gowns and slippers were doled out to patients whether they wanted them or not. They were later washed and sterilized on the hospital premises. In Derriford the patients brought their own nightwear from home. That was obviously another possible hygiene hazard, although I can see that wearing your own nightwear may be psychologically cheering. In Scandinavia the drab, uniform and shapeless pyjamas my previous patients had all worn made them look like indistinguishable pale brown or pink packets lying in their beds. It couldn't have been a comfortable thought, either, that you were wearing clothes that dozens of sick people, some of them now dead, had worn before you.

In Derriford, though, I found the nightwear actually helpful in assessing patients. Their choice often told a lot about their social background and personality, both of which can be useful in diagnosis. Frilly nightdress? See-through? Just covering the bottom? Long, long-sleeved, high-necked? Red satin pyjamas? Old-fashioned striped? Flowery? Flannel? Buttoned up, thick pyjamas? Old and frayed? Stained and unmended? Buttons missing? Carefully mended? Oh yes, you could tell a lot.

I hate the idea of pigeonholing people into social classes, which still seems so important in England, but in fact in medicine it can be very useful to know the social status of a person. If someone comes from a very deprived background, for instance, that person may be more likely to suffer from certain problems to do with lack of proper food, overcrowding, lack of hygienic conditions, etc. – though of course you can't generalize too much.

The patients were such a varied lot, anyway, but on the whole they tended to be much more talkative and joked much more than those in the Nordic countries. This was one of the big differences I'd always found between Finns and Swedes on the one hand and Brits on the other. Brits talked freely to strangers and they enjoyed wit, playing with words, irony and satire. If you go into a local shop in England, even where you are quite unknown, the shopkeeper is likely to crack a friendly joke across the counter; a stranger sitting opposite you in a café or train may do the same. These are certainly not cultural customs in Finland and Sweden. My patients at Derriford cracked jokes too, often when they were very ill and in pain. I would joke back and I found I got on with them very well. Nobody seemed to take much notice of my handicap, certainly not by questioning my competence. I had learned by now, when I first saw them, to say the mantra: 'Hello. I'm Victoria Webster, your doctor. You can hear I've got a slight speech defect. I hope it doesn't bother you too much.'

Nobody seemed to mind.

It was the same with my colleagues. They also accepted me and we laughed and joked a lot. Of course that helped us deal with a tough, serious and stressful job. For me, it also meant that at least one of my questions – would everyone in a big hospital accept me? – had been answered.

CHAPTER 31

Although the hospital accepted me, outside it could be a different story. I had at last found a cottage to rent in a village outside Plymouth. It was just off the moors, and the village itself might have posed for a 'pretty English village' poster, with a beautiful, huge old church at its centre, designed for those times gone by when everyone was a churchgoer. These days most such churches tend to be rather empty, with the congregation in a huddle together trying to keep warm. So I was surprised to find this one rather full, with a congregation of all ages and a service far removed from the traditional one. I didn't know anyone in the village yet and I hoped to meet people, so I went along to coffee after the service. A middle-aged woman, spotting a newcomer to welcome, came up to me and asked: 'Are you new here?'

'Yes,' I said. 'I've just moved in.'

She went on to ask the usual questions: my name, where I was living, and so on. As we talked, I noticed her voice was getting slower and a little louder. I knew the signs.

'And are you working?' she asked.

'Oh yes,' I said. 'I'm working at Derriford.'

She smiled kindly. 'A lot of people work there,' she said. 'What do you do?'

'I'm a doctor,' I said.

'A doctor?' she said politely. 'Er... how interesting.'

I could see that if I'd announced that I was the Queen, she would have had exactly the same reaction.

'And where is your family? Are they here too?'

'No,' I said. 'They live in Finland.'

Finland probably seemed to her on a par with the Queen. She said: 'Do you mean you're living alone? Oh dear.'

'Oh, I love my little cottage,' I said. 'Besides I don't have much time at home – the hours at the hospital are so long.'

'I wonder, my dear,' she said, 'I wonder if we might be of any help. We have a little group here that does outreach to people who... for people who...' She was floundering.

At this point we were both saved by a surgeon from the hospital coming up to me.

'Hello, Vicky,' he said. Then turning to the middle-aged woman, he added: 'Ah, I see, Molly, that you've already met Dr Webster.'

Rather soon afterwards, the woman made her escape and avoided me after that. People sometimes did when they realized they'd put their foot in it and they felt foolish.

I was so used to that sort of thing from outsiders that it didn't bother me much any longer, even if I didn't like being reminded each time how much my handicap showed. I knew she'd had the best of intentions.

I'd been surprised, though, to see the surgeon in the congregation – from what I'd seen in the Nordic countries, I'd concluded that not a lot of doctors there were churchgoers. I was glad to have been recognized in the church and acknowledged by a surgeon, because surgeons carry a lot of weight in society, just as they do in hospitals

– and very much so in Derriford. Something else I wasn't really used to there was the strict hierarchy among the hospital staff, affecting whether people socialized with each other or not. In Sweden and Finland, doctors of all ranks would sit together, and also with the nursing staff if they happened to be having lunch or a coffee break at the same time as they were. In Finland, all the doctors would sit together at the same table, and it was a great opportunity to discuss cases and problems. On the other hand, the nurses there didn't sit with us. 'That's the doctors' table,' they'd say, pointing to a good spot at the back of the room. In Derriford, not only did the nurses never sit with the junior doctors, but the junior doctors didn't sit with the consultants, not even for a coffee. And usually the different groups didn't socialize outside hospital hours either. People were rather surprised when at the start I went to the nurses' parties. I stopped after a while, though, as I thought it embarrassed them to have a doctor present. I was rather dismayed by these divisions and suspected it might have been a spin-off from the general class consciousness I'd found in England.

In England the nurses seemed anyway to have a different status from those in the Nordic countries, where nurses were felt to be fairly much the equals of the doctors, even if they did different jobs and got different salaries. That's very much in keeping with the general feeling of equality between people in Scandinavia and in Finland (with exceptions of course). But it seemed to me that a nurse in England was considered inferior. This is perhaps because the training of nurses and their responsibilities in the various countries is different. Some of the work that doctors do in Britain is often done by the nursing staff in Scandinavia, such as putting in stitches, taking blood or starting a drip, all of which they've been trained to do. So I was very surprised the first time I turned to a nurse in

Derriford to say: 'Could you stitch this up, please?' to have her answer: 'Sorry, we're not allowed to.'

Of course it would have helped the doctors very much if the nurses had been trained to perform some of the tasks, as it would have meant doctors could spend more time on other things.

As it was, the hours we had to work were appalling. Tom Beattie had warned me in Edinburgh it would be tough, but just how tough I really hadn't imagined. When I was on call on the surgery ward, for instance, I sometimes started on a Saturday at 8 a.m. and might carry on until 8 p.m. Monday. You were lucky if you got two to three hours' sleep meanwhile. I well remember coming off duty one evening and desperately ringing up Mum. I was sobbing with exhaustion.

'What's the matter?' she said at once.

'Oh, Mum,' I said. 'I just don't feel I can go on. I just can't do this!'

'What's happened?' she asked anxiously.

'Nothing,' I said. 'I'm just so, so tired. I've been on duty since Saturday morning. And I've been on surgery with about a hundred patients. And most of the time I was all alone and it was… it was… '

'Haven't you had any sleep?' she asked.

'No!' I wailed. 'It was too busy.'

'But it's Monday evening now!' she protested.

'Yes, I know,' I said. 'But I couldn't get away till now and I've had no food – there wasn't time – and I'm just so, so tired…'

'What are you going to do now?' she asked.

'Going home to bed,' I said.

'Driving?'

'How else?'

She'd know I'd be stubborn enough not to take a taxi.

'Well, you must promise me one thing,' she said. 'You've

got to have some food inside you before that. So promise me you'll stop off – however tired you are – either at a café or at a supermarket and get yourself something to eat and something hot to drink before you head off home. It won't be safe for you to be on the road otherwise – or for others. Promise!'

'OK,' I said reluctantly – but I knew she was right.

'And give me a quick call when you get home,' she said. 'So that I can be sure you made it.'

She rang me the next evening not only to check how I was but to give me sympathy and express her opinion of the system.

'It's bloody ridiculous,' she said. 'It's all wrong and it's not fair. It's not fair on you the doctors and it's not fair on the patients either. How can you possibly be expected to do good work in such circumstances?'

We couldn't, of course. In general, the enormous number of hours we put in a week meant that we only had time to shop, eat something fast, and sleep. A social life was out of the question. The physical and psychological effects on JHOs, SHOs and registrars was enormous. Our concentration and judgement were affected, and for me it also meant that my co-ordination suffered; but perhaps the more worrying thing was that our empathy for the patients decreased as we got more and more tired. It was, as my mother had said, a ridiculous situation – not fair to either the doctors or the patients. During the time that I was there, there were one or two well-publicized suicides by junior doctors in different parts of the country. I wasn't surprised. In the end, some time after I'd left the UK, the authorities did finally face up to the situation and the hours are somewhat better now.

At the same time as we worked, most of us were also studying for exams. My goal, as was that of my A&E colleague John, was to become a Fellow of the Royal

College of Physicians (FRCP), for which we first had to get our MRCP. Others were trying to become surgeons and get their FRCS (Fellow of the Royal College of Surgeons). You had to have one or the other to qualify as a specialist in A&E. The exams were in two parts – Part I was theoretical and Part II practical, and you had to pass the theory first. John had tried the exam before and failed.

'Part I is diabolical,' he said. 'It's all multiple choice questions – 300 of them – and each with three choices: correct, incorrect or blank.'

I moaned. 'I'm hopeless at multiple choice!' I said. 'Give me a patient to deal with and I'm fine; put me down in front of a multiple choice question and my brain turns to water. Even if I do know the answer, the choices make me think I don't.'

'That's not all,' he said. 'There's negative marking as well.'

'What's that?' I asked.

'You get points taken off for wrong answers,' he said. 'So those can cancel out the right ones and you can be left with miserable points at the end – or even minus points!'

'How horrific!' I said. 'Can't one do the practical first – surely that's what counts?'

'Nope,' he said. 'You've got to pass Part I or they'll never give you a shot at the practical.'

I was depressed. So was Mum when I told her. For seven years she had set the Finnish matriculation exam in English for all the schools in Finland. A major part of both the written exam and the listening comprehension exam had been made up of a passage followed by multiple choice questions. At the end of the seven years she'd given up. She said she was sick and tired of thinking up three wrong answers to every question when there was only one right one, and she thought it confusing to pupils even to see the possibility of a wrong answer. What's more, multiple choice exam techniques – as well as the art of guessing – are a skill that can be taught and learned. Although this of course doesn't mean that anybody who has learned them will pass, it certainly helps. Needless to say, I hadn't learned them.

Another problem was that the questions for the Part I MRCP exams were based on theory only and not on real-life situations. A lot were on chemistry and physics, which had been part of our training but were actually no longer relevant to daily clinical life. Both John and I were clinical doctors, with our student days rather far behind us. How we both wished that we could do the practical and show the examiners what we really could do!

The upshot was that I sat that wretched exam five times at a fee of £200 per go. I failed five times, too, which left me immensely depressed as well as much poorer. It wasn't much of a comfort that John, who I knew was a skilled and competent doctor, never passed either. The phone rang hot not only to Finland but also to Cornwall, where Mum's friend Anne had become a kind of surrogate mother to me and patiently listened to my moans, always encouraging and supporting me.

Despite all this, Derriford had confirmed several things for me. The most important were that yes, I was physically able to do clinical medicine; yes, the staff would accept me; and yes, the patients would accept me too. In the end, my handicap had made no difference, as they had assured me in Australia it would not: at last I felt an equal among equals.

It had also confirmed something else: that the future for me lay in A&E. In Derriford I also worked for periods on the surgery, gynaecology and obstetric wards. Just as had happened in Åland, the work there did not satisfy me as much as my work on A&E. Now, with hindsight, I wonder whether my consuming determination to go into A&E,

the specialty which perhaps entails most clinical practice of all, wasn't exactly because I had been so often warned that I wouldn't be able to do clinical work: on the same psychological grounds that opposition to any idea may cause people to become even keener on it. Maybe. On the other hand, I'd always loved action, doing things and interacting with people. Like some of the other members of my family, I had a taste for the dramatic, too, and A&E is where the drama is, although not usually to such a non-stop extent as the many TV series would suggest.

However, though I knew now beyond doubt that a specialty in A&E was what I wanted and something I could do, it was not enough. I was not a specialist in A&E yet, and with all those failures in the Part I exam of the MRCP, it didn't look as if I ever would be.

When we were about to take the exam for the fifth time, John had said to me: 'This is my last go. If I fail this, I'm going to give up.'

'What'll you do?' I asked.

'Try for a job in another hospital,' he said. 'After all, you don't have to become an FRCP to work in an A&E department and get a good job. You can be satisfied with being a middle grade doctor. OK, it's not so prestigious and you can't rise any higher and become a consultant, but that'll do me. What about you if you don't get through this time?'

'I just couldn't bear to go through all that again,' I said. 'Especially without a companion in my misery. But I don't know what I'd do. I can't quite bear to give up either. But my job here in Derriford is probably coming to an end too, so I don't know at all what I'm going to do.'

Maybe, I thought, I should follow John's example – but somehow I couldn't. Perhaps for me it was just one of those many challenges, yet another Everest, where I faced the impossible and was determined to overcome it, unable to

217

admit 'I can't do it.' Yet even I could see that my chances in the UK were slim. But what other choice did I have? Perhaps, I thought optimistically, something will turn up.

It did. I heard from my friend and colleague Sheila in Åland, who sent me an advertisement from a Swedish medical journal. Was I interested?

The ad was for a doctor in the A&E department of Södersjukhuset (the South Hospital) in Stockholm, which had started 'an A&E project' the previous year. I didn't know what that was exactly, but it sounded interesting. A Finnish friend of mine already had a job combining A&E and internal medicine at the Karolinska Hospital and we had both heard on the grapevine that the hospitals had been lobbying for a year now to get the Swedish National Board of Health and Welfare to make A&E a specialty of its own, as it already was in countries like the UK and the USA. That would be very exciting – if it ever happened.

I applied for the job.

CHAPTER 32

There were advantages to leaving, even though I'd been very happy in England and had much enjoyed Derriford and my colleagues in so many ways. I'd felt particularly lucky to have Iain Grant as my boss. I'd liked him the first time I'd met him at the interview and it was a joy to work under him. He had a wicked sense of humour as well as being kind and considerate to his patients and also to his staff. I learned a very great deal from him about being a doctor on A&E and shall always be grateful not only for that but for his support and encouragement when I most needed it – later as well. I was sorry I couldn't continue working under him but the unrelenting stress and pressures of all those hours had begun to wear me down. Tom Beattie in Edinburgh had been right to think I would need support from friends and relatives off duty, but there was hardly any off duty to be had.

Failing that wretched exam so many times had also begun to undermine my confidence once again. Did it mean that I was no good after all? That I didn't deserve to be in A&E medicine? No matter how many of my relatives and friends reassured me that I had never been any good at multiple choice exams, I thought they were just being kind. And now there'd come a chance of maybe getting where I wanted by another route.

Yes, I knew that in the past I'd said that never, ever would I work in Sweden, but with hindsight I knew that was a decision made in the immediate aftermath of my experience as a student at the Karolinska Institute. I did realize that things might be different now. Now I had a lot of varied experience and varied clinical work under my belt – and I'd proved I could do it.

I happened to have both Christmas and the New Year off that year and so was available for interviews. I applied to the Karolinska Hospital as well and had interviews there and at Södersjukhuset. The Karolinska Hospital said that they would give me a temporary job, as they wanted to see how we liked each other, as they tactfully put it. I imagined that this might be code for wanting to see if I could do the work, although I later learned that this was the custom at the Karolinska with any new employee. However, the Head of Medical Staff at Södersjukhuset, Thomas Arnhjort, offered me a permanent job on the spot. I unhesitatingly accepted and a little later I started working there in A&E.

The project was training doctors in all aspects of A&E irrespective of which specialist field the patient was admitted under. This was a broader system than the Karolinska Hospital's A&E with internal medicine and cardiology and more like the other European systems. There was some rivalry between these hospitals – both thought their own system would be the best for training doctors in A&E if the Swedish National Board of Health and Welfare should decide in the end to make it a specialty – and of course they both wanted to be the hospital that had trained the first A&E specialist. At this point, at the start of 2001, nobody could imagine it would not be until 2006 that it was finally decided.

Södersjukhuset was another huge hospital, with the largest A&E department in northern Europe, but luckily I was now used to that and all that it meant. The project, though, had its ups and downs. It had been sanctioned by the whole of the governing board of Södersjukhuset at the start, but even so it was extremely difficult to convince the heads of some of the other specialities at the hospital that A&E should be a specialty at all. Their reasons seemed to me both logical and illogical: A doctor needed to do a certain specialty all day and every day to keep up with developments in it; the juniors would never get enough expertise to become specialists; the teaching values of being on call for the juniors would be jeopardized; the system had always functioned perfectly well before, and so on. At times the animosity between the various heads of departments was very strong and some doctors working in the A&E department would find their work heavily criticized by a specialist in another department. The inevitable result was that the atmosphere became very strained and uncomfortable to work in.

I want to stress, though, that I was spared all the attacks. Nothing was ever aimed at me personally: on the contrary, I seemed well liked and would often be told what a good clinician I was, irrespective of specialty. I was immensely grateful for this and it came as a huge relief when I thought of other episodes in my past. However, my feelings were completely on the side of my own department, and I was depressed by the bad working atmosphere that the squabbles had created there.

By the beginning of 2003, I started to realize that I'd now worked for more than eight years after becoming a doctor. It was high time I became a specialist in something that would then enable me to work permanently in A&E, as it usually took about five years to get a specialty of any kind. My choice of specialty was rather limited, too. Anything that involved operations was obviously out because of my handicap, and anyway I really had no experience of operations except for assisting in them and sewing up wounds and cuts. I'd discovered, too, that I wouldn't really be happy in the world of the General Practitioner. That really only left internal medicine.

I started asking about specializing in internal medicine at Södersjukhuset and sent the department my papers. The seniors there noted that they showed I had already had a lot of experience in internal medicine, but they thought it would still take me three to five years, doing internal medicine alone, before they would consider me a specialist in it. It would mean I would do very little A&E at all during that time, as I would only be on call for the internal medicine cases. I wasn't too pleased at the thought, as I now knew for sure that A&E was my niche.

I sent in the same papers to Dag Nyman at the Åland Central Hospital. He studied them and obviously took my experience into account, because he decided that it would take a year to a year and a half before he could sign the necessary document. Obviously Åland was the place for me to try to get my internal medicine specialty. I was delighted, as at least this solved my problems for the moment. I wanted to keep my future options open, though, so I asked Södersjukhuset for eighteen months' leave. Shortly after that, I found myself back in Mariehamn once more, this time on the internal medicine ward. At the same time I was on call once or twice a week for A&E, so I kept my hand in there, so to speak.

Just before my time on internal medicine was to finish, a job opened up for a temporary second-in-command in the A&E department in Åland. I had earlier found out that the strained relationships between the other departments and the A&E in Södersjukhuset still existed. Going back to that did not seem a tempting prospect. There had also still been no decision about making A&E a specialty in Sweden. I decided to ask for an extension of my leave-of-absence from there and to apply for the Åland job. At least it would add an upgrade to my CV even if it was temporary, and there was always the possibility that the job might later become a permanent one if the doctor who'd held it up to now decided not to return. Södersjukhuset understood and gave me the extension.

So there I was back in familiar little Mariehamn with my old friends and colleagues, working under Jan Österberg again and with the nurses with whom I'd worked so amicably before. I was very cheered by the welcome I got from everybody and enjoyed being back and in a way 'at home'.

The job lasted for a year and a bit. During that time I got my specialty in internal medicine, which was one of the three that entitled you to work in A&E in Finland. The former second-in-command in A&E in Mariehamn by now had decided not to return, but his job had not yet been advertised. Meanwhile, another possible candidate for it, an intelligent and very conscientious man who was actually originally from Åland, went to work in the Mariehamn internal medicine department for six months in my place. I knew the job would eventually be advertised; I thought the choice would most probably be between me and the Ålander; I did not want to return to Sweden yet until it was advertised and when I then could apply – what should I now do in between?

I went to work for three months in Helsinki at the Maria Hospital, where I was both in A&E and on the wards. The hospital, which had a great many elderly patients, was desperately overcrowded and equally short of staff. We could have as many as sixty patients in the A&E department in one day. It was quite a shock after my little Åland hospital.

In Maria, though, just as in Derriford, Södersjukhuset and Åland, my handicap was disregarded. I would still produce my mantra, though: 'Hello, I'm Victoria Webster. I'm your doctor. I have a speech handicap, but I hope it doesn't bother you.'

It never did seem to bother anyone. Not, that is, if you disregard those few whose objection was that I was a woman. Most female doctors had the occasional objection that they were not male – sometimes on religious grounds – and some people could be convinced that the women couldn't be doctors but must be nurses. But that sort of thing could happen to any female doctor and in fact even these days I get mistaken for a nurse almost daily. On the contrary, my handicap could now count in my favour: there were several patients who had answered the mantra by replying: 'No, I want you as my doctor. If you've got this far with a handicap, you must be better than the rest.'

I don't think that's a valid argument, but it was certainly cheering.

During the three months at Maria, the job as second-in-command at the A&E department in Mariehamn came up. I applied, even if by now I was not totally convinced that I wanted it. If I got it, I would be honour bound to stay there for a few years at least, and that meant not going anywhere where I could get that longed-for specialty in A&E at last. In the end, I think it was pride – not to be rejected, to be the chosen one – that was the main reason I wanted the job. But the other main candidate had a lot going for him and I was certainly not at all confident that I would be chosen.

It was several months before we heard the result. I didn't get it.

CHAPTER 33

The very next day, I got an email from Södersjukhuset saying that my period of secondment was up and did I want to return? At the same time, it mentioned that the Swedish National Board was once again discussing whether to make A&E a supplementary specialty and was now drawing up a new set of requirements. It looked as if the decision might be in place and the requirements known by January of the next year. What's more, the problems that A&E had had at the hospital seemed to have been resolved, and the atmosphere was once again a happy one.

It was now March 2006. Without hesitation, I packed my bags once more and headed for Stockholm.

July came and – yes, A&E was now a supplementary specialty. It had to come after the candidate had first got a full specialty, but of course by now I'd already got mine in internal medicine. I clocked up a few more courses of various kinds, and then my supevisor and I went through the requirements, matching them against my qualifications, experience, courses, etc. Two of us at Södersjukhuset were very close to meeting them – almost there. So too were some at the Karolinska Hospital and perhaps elsewhere in Sweden – who knew? The Karolinska Hospital and

Södersjukhuset had often been rivals before and now were once again. Which hospital would be the first to have a specialist doctor in A&E in Sweden? In fact this meant throughout Scandinavia and Finland, as it was only Sweden that had as yet introduced the specialty.

My supervisor encouraged me to send in my papers. We'd heard by now that nine other doctors had turned in their papers and that all nine had been turned down – we didn't know why. Did they have some course missing? Was there something else in their papers that didn't meet the examiners' requirements? Again, we didn't know. At any rate, we knew that the answer would take a long time in coming, whatever it was – possibly not until Christmas – so after I'd posted my papers I actually managed to put it out of my mind.

That was in February 2007. By now it was June and I was due to take my holiday. As I had done for the past few years, I was going to spend the first two weeks of it doing voluntary work as a doctor at a sailing and water sports summer camp for children with allergy problems. It was by the sea in the country, the kids were fantastic and so were my colleagues, and I always enjoyed myself thoroughly.

As usual, I did my packing at the last minute, hurling country clothes, swimming things and suitable shoes into the back of the car. The post came while I was doing it and I threw that into the back of the car as well.

I opened it later at a stop en route to the camp. There was a big, thickish envelope among the rest and I wondered idly what it was.

Out of it I pulled a stiff paper. It said:

*The Swedish National Board of Health and Welfare declares in
accordance with Swedish Law that the medical practitioner*

VICTORIA WEBSTER

has been granted the qualification as a Specialist in
ACCIDENT AND EMERGENCY MEDICINE.

I had got my specialty in A&E. Sweden's first.

EPILOGUE (Diana's)

Very recently, Spratty/Victoria and I went on a mother–daughter trip to Florence for a week. We were staying in a *pensione* in the hills above Florence just below Fiesole. It was a delightful, old-fashioned place where I had stayed several times before and which I knew Spratty would enjoy too. We would take the bus down to Florence in the early morning and then up again after lunch, arriving footsore, hot and delightfully surfeited with madonnas. We would have a siesta in our cool room and then get up in the late afternoon in time for a read on the terrace, shaded by wisteria, looking down on Florence in the valley below, the perfect and almost unreal dome of the cathedral shimmering above the haze until the setting sun touched it into a vibrant reddish gold.

This particular late afternoon we had taken postcards to write and by early evening we were sipping chilled white wine as we wrote. A party of elderly English people had arrived that day and were sitting at the nearby table drinking very large whiskies. There were two couples whom I identified immediately as belonging to a certain type of English people who used to be called 'the gentry' or 'county people'. No doubt the two men had been to public schools of some kind and the women had probably once had servants. They were well-bred ladies and gentlemen who spoke in well-bred voices. They would, I thought, be likely to pigeon-hole people according to what school they went to, who they knew, to whom they were related. It was a type I had been familiar with in my younger years in England. Some of them could be admirable, men and women of great dignity, honour and integrity; some tiresome and boring; some so devoid of understanding of anything outside their own sphere as to seem from another age.

These two couples also spoke rather loudly: I supposed that being in a foreign country they assumed they were surrounded by foreigners who couldn't understand English or, more charitably, maybe it was that at least one of them was deaf. As I paused to think of the address for one of my cards, I saw that they were looking our way and apparently talking about us.

'I think that woman behind you must be from the Something Institute,' said Wife One. 'Look, she's writing.'

I knew that there was a large research institute for cultural studies of some kind somewhere near the *pensione* and, with my university background, instantly supposed they were referring to that. As the man turned to see who his wife was speaking about, I though it might save them possible future embarrassment if I let them know we could understand whatever they said. I went into well-bred-voice mode: 'No,' I smiled at them both. 'We live in Finland. We're here on holiday so that I could show my daughter Florence for the first time.'

'Ah, I see,' said Husband One, looking a trifle taken aback.

'Oh yes,' said Wife One, understandingly. 'We took my brother-in-law to Paris last year, you know. We thought it would be nice for him to see it. But of course he couldn't read or write.'

'Oh, I'm sure he must have enjoyed it,' I said politely, not understanding at all what the connection could be, and thinking she had only half heard what I had said.

The conversation was interrupted by the dinner bell. The couples got up and made their way to the dining-room, while Spratty and I gathered up our postcards and pens.

'What a weird conversation,' I said. 'What on earth was that woman on about?'

Spratty laughed. Experience had got her there long before I had.

'I think she was demonstrating that she had done a good deed as well,' she said.

And then I realized. I had not identified Spratty as 'the woman behind you', as to me she was still a girl, my daughter, but what the woman had meant was 'that woman with a handicap' and 'Look! She can actually write!' I went on from that to assume that the Something Institute must be a place she knew which took the mentally handicapped and sometimes managed to teach them to read and write.

The old fury, long buried, surged up inside me. It was not allayed by the events next evening. We were again on the terrace, again sipping our delicious white wine, but this time reading. I saw with some relief that the English couples with the large whiskies were now at a more distant table, where they could not be heard. The dinner bell sounded, but Spratty was just finishing a chapter and so continued reading. The English party got up and passed us to go down to the dining-room. As they did so, Husband Two stopped by us and said to Spratty: 'Ah, you're reading, I see. I wonder what you are reading.'

He lent over her and took the book out of her hand. I was astounded, as to take a book out of a lady's hand is definitely not a well-bred thing to do.

'Ah,' he said, looking at the book and seeming somewhat at a loss. '*Northanger Abbey*. How interesting!'

'Yes,' said Spratty politely. 'It's one of Jane Austen's novels I haven't read. It was in the library here.'

'Oh,' he said. 'Jane Austen. How nice.'

He handed it back and moved on. What had he expected? Large print? Simple words and sentences? I imagine so. I regretted that it hadn't been something like *Developments in the Treatment of Patients with Acute Aphasia* or even her previous night's detective story in Swedish, which would then have enabled me to say: 'Yes, isn't she lucky? She's trilingual.'

I was so angry I could hardly control myself and all through dinner mentally rehearsed things I might say to them. I devoutly and unworthily hoped that one of them would suffer a heart attack during their stay, which would enable Spratty to say: 'I'm a doctor. Let me deal with it.'

Not that they would have believed her, of course.

The contrast next morning with the señora who ran the hotel was marked. I knew her from before, and she was telling me about her son, who had asthma.

I said: 'My daughter's a doctor. She knows a lot about asthma – she's asthmatic herself.'

'Ah!' said the señora instantly. 'Perhaps she could give me some advice. Do you think I could ask her?'

'Of course you could,' I said. 'If she can help in any way, she certainly will.'

She did.

Thankfully, we never saw the English party again and when I had calmed down, I considered that at least one thing the episode showed was how far Spratty had come in being able to deal with the reactions of ignorant, unthinking and prejudiced people. But my heart still goes out to the brother-in-law who was taken to Paris even though he could not read or write. I wondered what assumptions had been made about him all his life.

In retrospect, the Florence story illustrated something I had not realized before: that Spratty had acquired the ability to brush off the prejudice and assumptions she still met in a way that I had not managed to do even then. The scenes in that Italian *pensione* roused in me exactly the same emotions I had had during similar scenes in her childhood: fury, resentment, pain, the frustrated desire to defend and protect. And also anger with myself for not being able to protest against it, to speak out instantly. What kept me silent? A British sense of not wanting to create a scene? The idea of 'grin and bear it'? Conventional politeness? Ridiculous! And yet, just as in the old days, I had felt that if she herself could treat it so tolerantly and with such rueful good humour, then so should I. She was no longer shocked or even surprised. Presumably it happened so often that she no longer took much notice, she could bear it. But presumably too this was because she had achieved what she wanted, and because inside herself she knew that she could prove them wrong if she thought it worth her while. What then of all those others who had not achieved their goals and were still so vulnerable?

And is Dr Victoria Webster no longer vulnerable? Has she really come out of all her experiences unscathed? I don't think so. Despite her ultimate and triumphant achievement of her goal, I still feel she has been deeply scarred in one way. All the praise or the demonstration of her undoubted skill and ability cannot even now quite remove her self-doubt and lack of complete confidence in herself. This is not because of her physical handicap, something that her mind and body overcame long ago – it is the result of other people's reactions to it. In particular, her treatment by some of her classmates at school, at the most impressionable age, instilled in her a belief of being unable to do things, and of being subnormal even in intelligence. This was then reinforced by her treatment at the hands of some of her teachers when she was a medical student. Even if she has suppressed and denied this belief, it is there lurking in the background, undermining her. In other words, one handicap has been replaced by another, simply because of the ways others have behaved towards her.

What I have learned through her is that the first thing anyone who has a handicap needs, no matter what or however mild or severe the handicap may be, is love and a secure background, together with positive encouragement coming from a sincere belief that problems can be overcome. Close behind comes the need not to be treated as 'different', and that no assumptions should be made about what a handicapped person cannot or will not be able to do. The emphasis should always be on what they can or might do, not on what they can't. Yet the negative attitude is far more common than the positive one. Even friends will often say to Spratty: 'It's remarkable what you've done in spite of your handicap.'

She will always answer: 'It's not 'in spite of', it's 'with it'. I wouldn't be what I am without it – it's part of me, the whole package.'

A handicap is automatically assumed to be something bad: all the words for it like 'handicap', 'disability', 'impaired', suggest this. The emphasis is on 'can't' from the outset. Yet nobody, not even experts, can say with absolute certainty, especially in our technical age, what a handicapped person can or will be able to do in the future. Many have confounded the pessimistic predictions.

Above all, the public needs educating on the subject to prevent the discrimination that exists today. Not so very long ago, anybody black was perceived by white people to be 'primitive', unintelligent, a non-achiever, even sub-human. The education of the public and many brave campaigners, not least black people themselves, have dispelled this idea for the majority, if not all. Again not so long ago, women used to be in much the same position – a woman was still thought in the early twentieth century to be automatically inferior to and less intelligent than a man; example and the education of the public has to some extent changed that view in the western world. There is roughly the same assumption about the handicapped: they are probably sub-normal or at least destined to be non-achievers.

All three of the categories have in common that they are immediately identifiable as being different from the norm – whatever that norm may be. All of them have been able to arouse prejudice from being so identified. All of them have had campaigns fought about them over the last sixty years or so to make them more integrated into 'normal' society. Some of the campaigns have been more successful than others; but still all too often when one of the people in these categories is promoted to a high position one can hear murmurs about it not being a matter of competence but of being 'PC', of it looking good on paper. As Spratty says, if she was black she'd be offered jobs all the time, because she would usefully tick the three boxes in one go: black, female and handicapped.

Historically, what creates a change in public attitudes and acceptance of differences is, and has always been, example and education. It is in the hope that attitudes can be altered, even if gradually, that we have written this book. It has not been easy to write. We have had to revive memories and feelings which both of us would have preferred to forget. Living them over again has often caused tears, and we have frequently had to stop and change the subject to something less painful. Yet we think that Victoria's story might encourage people to see the handicapped in another light, and to realize the assumptions and prejudices which may exist quite unconsciously in their own minds. We especially hope that parents will help, by example, to instil a lack of prejudice in their own children, and to combat bullying and teasing in school.

It can be done. This story demonstrates that there are also people who are able to see beyond an exterior handicap. They are those without whom Spratty would never have achieved her goal. A few of them must certainly have doubted her ability to do so, at least at the start, but in no way were they going to discourage her by word or look. On the contrary: if they could help her, they would and did. It is to all these people – family, friends and strangers alike – that we dedicate this book.

Diana Webster